Notes / Exercises

I WANTED THE WEDDING, NOT THE MARRIAGE

You wanted the day.
You weren't ready for the life!

LaVetta Price

I WANTED THE WEDDING, NOT THE MARRIAGE

You wanted the day.
You weren't ready for the life!

LaVetta Price

ARPress
45 Dan Road Suite 15
Canton MA 02021
　Hotline:　　1(888) 821-0229
　Fax:　　　　1(508) 545-7580

Ordering Information:
Quantity sales. Special discounts are available on quantity purchases by corporations, associations, and others. For details, contact the publisher at the address above.

Printed in the United States of America.

ISBN-13:　　Softcover　　979-8-89676-656-8
　　　　　　　eBook　　　979-8-89676-657-5

Library of Congress Control Number: 2025927709

This book is dedicated to the memory of my husband
Lamone Budda Price may you forever rest in peace.
A marriage, and friendship that no one could break no
matter our challenges.

TABLE OF CONTENTS

FOREWORD

MICHAEL BART MATHEWS

Lavetta Price shares her compelling story about her personal experience with relationships and marriage. She discusses her happiness, trials, tribulations, setbacks, and many unbelievable truths as your guide to understanding that you (man or woman) do not have to suffer in silence because of the complexities of marriage. Lavetta is not against marriage because she had been married for over thirty years before divorcing. This book is not about man-bashing! It's about "TO TELL THE TRUTH" from the woman who experienced her truth. She made it her mission to share a multitude of relationship issues that she experienced, and countless other women (to some degree) have experienced some of her stories.

Ladies, as you turn the pages of this must-read book, you will discover that you are not alone! **Men**, as you turn the pages of this must-read book, you will automatically self-reflect as to what type of man you really are within your relationship or marriage. This self-reflection is a powerful tool that can lead to personal growth and a deeper understanding of your role in the relationship. Lavetta will share her insights on relationships, the art of marriage, spirituality, and specific bible verses from the Higher Power (God) that will make the point and bridge the stories pertaining to earthly man & woman from God's teaching on marriage.

Starting with the fairy tale whirlwind romance before marriage that some experience while others get married with no fanfare whatsoever. You will read about the complexities of merging men and women (marriage), as well as the many give-and-takes required for both partners to make the union work. From living a single life to cohabitating under one roof. Having children, running the household, working partners/spouses and one spouse trying to change the other to fit his or her version of how the other should be. All of the abovementioned factors (and more) are causes for long-lasting love and marriage or unsettling relationships leading to dislike, distrust, anger, separation, and divorce.

During my research, I found that 673,989 people in the United States were divorced in 2022. That's 2.4 divorces per 1,000. In that same year, more than 2 million marriages took place. Also, in 2022, 61.44 million married couples were in the United States. My research also disclosed that 69% of women are likely to initiate a divorce, and 31% of men initiate a divorce.

Why are these numbers important? Inside the pages of this book, you will read about different pathways that lead to divorce. The above numbers are proof positive that an alarming number of women and men initiate divorce proceedings, while many couples stay married despite their differences.

Lavetta Price will share some of the many reasons (not all) divorces happen. For example, lack of commitment or sexual marital infidelity, trust issues, financial issues, weight gain, post-honeymoon is over, now back to reality syndrome. Also, verbal abuse, mental abuse, physical abuse, and substance (drugs/alcohol) abuse are factors.

Another factor that causes divorces is differences in religious beliefs or the lack thereof.

In closing, I have a question for you. Do you know the difference between a roommate and a soul mate? The answer can be found inside this tell-all book by Lavetta Price.

As a married man for over 26 years to my wife, Robbie S. Mathews, we experienced the ebb and flow of marriage throughout our union. I have often been told that because of my life-long, unwavering support for women, I took it upon myself to make it my lifelong mission to love, honor, respect, and support all women, especially my wife. During my many conversations with men and women, I discovered that men were brought up to be hard: don't show your feelings, don't show your emotions, don't cry, and be tough. That same upbringing is what some men bring into their marriage. And that's a problem! Well, men, that's not what women (in my opinion) want from a man.

I am writing this foreword supporting Lavetta Price's story, which depicts how males and men are different. Guys, all males are not men! I am supported by fellow like-minded men who understand the true value and leadership women (married or single) bring to the table. I also support our gift from God, which is the empowering WOMEN in our lives.

Lavetta believes in the security and sanity of a good marriage because it's not that "Boys Will Be Boys"; it comes from the saying "Men, Not Males, Will Be Men."

From the words/lyrics of Bobby Womack: "Fellows, do you mind if I talk to you for a minute? Sometimes we have a tendency, or we forget what a woman needs every now and then. That is, if you want to keep your thang together. Do the things that keeps a smile on her face – "A Woman's Gotta Have it-She Got To Know That She's Needed Around-She Wants To Know That She Not Walking On Shakey Ground."

This book is a must-read for men and women alike!

Michael Bart Mathews
International Speaker
Author of # 1 New Book Release, Fifty-Two Shades of Inspiration
Author of Pathway To Trauma Recovery: Transform Pain Into Power Overcome The Mystery
Author of Financially Speaking: The Best Improvement Starts With Self-Improvement
Executive Producer of The Living W.E.A.L.T.H.Y. with Robbie Streaming TV Show on JD3TV.
info@tmeginc.com

INTUITION

Britannica Dictionary definition of INTUITION. 1. [noncount]: a natural ability or power that makes it possible to know something without any proof or evidence: a feeling that guides a person to act a certain way without fully understanding why. Intuition was telling her that something was very wrong.

They say that women have the deepest intuition, but I also believe men have it as well. It's in all of us it protects us from harm, danger, our spiritual inner guide. We, as women, use it more when it comes to men, our husband, that radar kicks in.

We always feel it when we are worried or unsure of something, a warning to either go or stay. When someone is not right. I would always get those feelings when my husband was messing around. Or if he was in harm's way. That goes for my kids as well. But do we always listen to the warnings? Nope, we don't. I have had many of them. And when you don't listen to the warnings, we pay dearly sometimes to a point of no return.

Story time: Two weeks before my wedding, I was at my mother-in- law's house and all his brothers was there with their girlfriends. At the time in 91 when we got married it, was three of us that we're going to get married within that year. His mom did stuff for everybody in their wedding except for me. She didn't buy anything that contributed to my wedding. And she let it be known that she wasn't going to do not one thing or give one penny. The first marriage was umm if I'm not mistaken, it was his oldest brother and then us and then his other brother that lived out of state. We were at her house, and everybody was in the living room and we started having this discussion and so she did something for everybody's wedding except for mine.

She would say she didn't know why the hell he was marrying me in the first damn place because she didn't want him to marry me. She wanted him to marry his first baby Mama so anyway we were all in the living room and she started saying that she wasn't going to get nothing for my wedding now mind you she got the other two that got married she catered one of their receptions she got everything for it and then his older brother she brought her wedding cake now when they came to mine she told me she wasn't doing a damn thing for mine that she didn't even know if she was coming and that mine wasn't going to be nothing but a gang banger party anyway.

So funny part of it was my wedding was the best wedding out of all of them it was more classy it was very elegant it was a black and white affair going back to the discussion so when she told me that she wasn't doing a damn thing for my wedding she wasn't getting me anything at that time I didn't need anything anyway I said well you don't have to buy me anything or get anything for our wedding because my mom and my aunt already paid for everything the only thing that I had left to pay for was my bouquet and I and at the time I only owed $100 so I didn't need your money and so then she told me that she wasn't even going to come and so I told her I didn't give a damn if she came or not because she's not my mother and that my mother was going to be there and that that's all that matters to me and that she wasn't coming to representing me she was coming to represent her son and so if she didn't show up it would hurt him more than it would hurt me and so you know everybody was on the couch going ooh and ah and was like damn she's saying that and you know she was telling me isn't nobody going to be there but gang banger and my wedding wasn't going to be shit. Mind you my husband was a gang member and one of his brothers was too.

I asked how you are going to talk about my family being in a gang when your kids are doing the same thing. Sitting on your couch all colored up. And all of this stuff now mind you the decor was Immaculate our food was top of the line my wedding cake was made by the Queen Mary chef we had a ten tier black and white cake with real ribbons and it was simply beautiful my dress was tailor made I even helped made it was um off the line of Bob Mackie and my wedding ring was to die for no he didn't pay for it I did because I wanted a nice ring and he couldn't afford the ring that I wanted so I bought it for myself but anyhow so anyway after that argument I mean that argument was really heated and my husband fiancé at the time didn't step in didn't say nothing didn't interfere he let his mother talk to me like shit he didn't say a word I was embarrassed to say the least in front of everybody.

And so I didn't understand why I was the only one that she didn't want to do anything because after all we were already had two kids by him he was already living with me back and forth and he was OK and had been together already 6 years. Or more I forgot. You know but again she still wanted him with his first Filipino baby Mama and she was in love with her and in saying that even after we got married 20 years later she still had her picture up in her cabinet not a picture of her and him not a picture of him but a picture of her umm so going back to the wedding so I didn't talk to him for two weeks I didn't even know if he was going to show up or not so I didn't talk to him I didn't do anything his tuxedo was ordered but I didn't pay for it the wedding was already paid for and done so if he didn't show up we were just going to have one big ass party.

So I didn't know I actually really truly didn't know if he was going to show up until the day of the wedding and so anyway when I'm speaking on intuition the day before my matron of honor who was or my maid of honor I think my cousin was a matron of honor of my maid of honor she was his brother's ex-girlfriend fiancé my brother's ex-girlfriend she was messing with my husband too.

So she just had them all and so then that's a whole another story in itself but anyhow so she called me and told me that she didn't have her dress and so then I said well where is it I'll pay for it cause I want you in my wedding because at the time she was like a sister to me we did everything together you know we did literally everything together meaning we shared men too. unknowingly. But anyway, so then she says no it's OK, I'm just going to come to the wedding, and I'll see you there. She couldn't stand there because she knew she was fucking my soon to be husband. She said, "Well because I don't have a dress and it's too late and really, I didn't get a chance to order it. Anything to make an excuse not to be in it. But I wasn't having it, I wanted my play sister at my wedding.

So I didn't even know that she didn't even have the dress and so then so then I told her well there's something in your closet cause she dressed well so I wasn't caring I said just wear something in your closet I don't care you're like you're like my sister and I want you in my wedding I don't care what you wear and so then the day of the wedding uh she came and so she was still adamant about not being in the wedding but I didn't know at the time why and so then when she oh I made her be in my wedding anyway oh she stood up there with me, and it wasn't until later on that night that everything would change.

The wedding went well his mother did show up he showed up his mother was very pretty she actually looked at better at my wedding than she did at the other two son's wedding she actually looked really really pretty and he showed up, looking good too so I guess that was her contribution to our wedding because she made sure that he got his tuxedo because I still to that up till that day didn't pay for it his hair was cut he looked amazing.

So I was relieved that I wasn't going to be embarrassed that I was not going to get stood up at the altar and so then the day went nice it went the way I wanted it and planned it was simply beautiful everybody was beautiful. but our pictures didn't reflect pure happiness if you see our pictures um they didn't seem like unity actually.

After the wedding she grabbed me and she gave me a hug and she said I love you Lavetta and I told her no you don't get away from me because you just told me two weeks ago that you didn't know why the hell he was marrying me in the 1st place so how are you going to come back and tell me that you love me when you didn't even want him to marry me so I didn't believe that I stayed away from her mostly at the wedding but was cordial and nice and I was glad that she showed up so.

Anyway moving forward um the wedding the reception was over we had a hotel room and for some reason I don't know it didn't go through or cancelled or something other we ended up on at a motel not a hotel but a motel and so then when I changed out of my wedding dress and got into something pretty and sexy my we was we started doing it and I got this feeling that came over me and so then so then when we started having sex I just had this weird feeling that something wasn't right and sure enough the next morning it wasn't right.

I have found out that my best friend the girl they didn't want to get the her wedding outfit was uh fucking my husband that's when I found out that it's been going on for a while I have I had other hints again I didn't want to believe it different things that they have done and stuff like that but I kind of shun it off as of you know no not her no she wouldn't do that but they were and so not only did I find out that the next day that they were fucking.

I also found out that my mother-in-law and my sister-in-law made a bet of $1.00 that my marriage wouldn't last one year so when I found that out I went up to my sister-in-law and gave her a dollar and told her that I was paying her fee I don't know which way she was betting on I don't know if she was betting it was going to last longer a year or she was in agreement with her that it wasn't going to last a year. But despite me finding out that he was messing with my best friend, I was determined to prove that we were going to last over a year. Not only that, but my husband also went to jail the next day for warrants. That's when he found out that I knew what he had been doing.

I didn't drink but I went and got me some Cisco and got drunk the whole world was spinning. His best friend and mother took care of me. stupid maybe yes and trust and believe I paid for not listening to my intuition I end up staying over 35 years, but I paid I truly paid for not listening because it didn't stop. He kept going and going with lots of other friends but I loved him. I'd be a fool to sit up here and say it that I didn't, and I made a vow to God and to him for better for worse richer for poor all that I stayed true. but he never did.

So, on the contrary that's what I get for not listening to my intuition because my intuition told me that it wasn't right and then God even put it in my face of the things that was being done and saying and yet I still stay. So, I say that please think lots of times before you take that step and listen to the red flags, don't marry too young, get it out and your system be ready. Whether not ready kids or not don't do it. Because in the end you lose yourself, time, money, things you can never get back.

The only thing that I wouldn't change would be my babies my kids if I didn't stay married I wouldn't have all the beautiful kids that I have today I probably would have still only had the two and I know that my life would have been different but at the same time I have no regrets I have 7 beautiful amazing children and 12 grandkids out of our union.

I'm have to be all the way transparent he still was messing with her after we got married, I found out then she end up getting in trouble and going to jail. see karma is a bitch. she even got married a couple of other times and in her marriages, she was beaten by her husbands, even ended up messing around with her real sister so everything that she was doing to me was done back to her more so worse. Not to say I condone men beating on women, I DON'T. but I am not going to say I felt sorry for her either. That's the human side of me. She didn't care about my feelings so why should I gave a damn what happened to her. so, I didn't have to do anything saying that, you know what it says vengeance is mine saith the Lord. Romans 12:19-21 King James Version (KJV) Dearly beloved, avenge not yourselves, but rather give place unto wrath: for it is written, Vengeance is mine; I will repay, saith the Lord. Therefore, if thine enemy hunger, feed him; if he thirsts, give him drink: for in so doing thou shalt heap coals of fire on his head.

Romans 12:19-21 Never take your own revenge... - Bible.com

Bible.com

https://www.bible.com HYPERLINK "https://www.bible.com/ bible/compare/ROM.12.19-21#:~:text=Romans%20 12%3A19-21%20King,of%20fire%20on%20his%20head." › bible › compare › ROM.12.19-21

You know I had to back that one up with proof. LOL. Really that is why I didn't do a lot of tit for tat because I knew that one day God would get those who hurt me. Turn the other cheek they say. But I am human and sometimes you must let a bitch know that's why I was going to slice that hoe.

So I say this to say that don't just do what you think that's right if God give you an sign that something isn't right listen to it research it find out what the root cause of what you're really feeling it's OK to not go through with something that's a lifelong change just because you spent the money have a hell of a party what's more embarrassing is going through pain for not listening that hurts more than calling it off and moving on with your life.

I should have took the signs and moved on with my life but I didn't and give and saying that given if I had the signs and had to do it over again I wouldn't do it the way that I did my last name became a price and I said I paid the price to be a price now I'm ready to get rid of it I don't want to be a price anymore it hurts too much sadly I can't even say it was all worth it only thing that was worth it was I knew my baby's love me even if he didn't fully.

I don't believe that he didn't love me I just believed that he didn't know how he wasn't taught correctly as far when it came to relationships. I had him when he was a boy all the way up to a man. so when I say that I'm saying it as we went through a lot of learning and through that learning the first wife always seemed to be the one to take the blunt of the pain and the learning curve so when he gets to the next woman he knows what to do and what not to do because he doesn't fear of losing her because he does better I think if we were to remarried and do it all over again things would have been a lot different better because he's no longer a boy he became a different man.

I DO

When we find our person, the one we want to take it to the next step the marriage. Some have children first, live with them first all part of life and everyone situation is different. But the end goal if you're seeking it, is marriage. Commitment everyone wants to belong to someone even if they must share. Commit to me let me know you value me enough to want me as your own. Loving as you love yourself.

Life is hard enough and going though it alone is even harder. We were never meant to be alone. When Adam was made and he was lonely, needing love and someone to be with. God saw that it was not good for Adam to be alone and decided to create a suitable helper for him (Genesis 2:18). This shows God's concern for Adam and His understanding of human nature. He knew that Adam needed companionship and someone to share his life with. Christian Pure https://www.christianpure.com

Genesis 2:18-24 English Standard Version 2016 (ESV) But for Adam there was not found a helper fit for him. So the LORD God caused a deep sleep to fall upon the man, and while he slept took one of his ribs and closed up its place with flesh. Then the LORD God said, "It is not good for the man to be alone

Bible.com

I was watching 90-day fiancée one of their series and Brandon's mother made a commit to his bride to be. not quoting verbatim but she said something to the sort that when you get married you should marry not because you can live with that person, but you marry because you can't live without them. I thought that was the best way of putting why you should marry that person. And it was beautiful to say, and it was the truth. When you marry because you can live with that person that is not love in its entirety it's a roommate. We split everything right down to the soap. But when you marry because you can't live without that person you become as one whole like Adam felt when God gave him Eve.

Adam couldn't live without Eve, and he proved it by not following Gods one rule. What he does Following his wife. Now I understand the concept. But I am mad at Adam because if God gave you one wife don't you think he would have given him another one if she was bad? Hell, men have different wives now what was to be the difference in his time? I am mad at Eve too stupid women that goes to show we do need men as our leaders. We're much more gullible than men. If it wasn't for her, we would not have all this stuff going on as a woman. Our pain is much worse than a man all because of Eve. It also shows us how powerful the beauty, the pussy is for men. They too can't live without it and that is why so easily manipulated by women all since Eve. THE TRUE POWER OF A WOMEN. Was proven since the very beginning of time.

What do we really want from a husband? And what does the Bible say the husband should be? A Christian husband should love his wife as he does himself and always protect her from all harm (Eph. 5:25–29). He should do his best to "nurture and cherish" his wife in the love of Christ as he would his own flesh and tend to her spiritual, emotional, intellectual, and physical needs (Eph. 5:29; Col. Jan 25, 2017)

Core Christianity https://corechristianity.com

What a husband should be according to the Bible?

Husbands should not be harsh with their wives. Husbands should honor their wives. That husbands should love their wives as their own bodies, also as Christ loved the church, and be willing to sacrifice themselves for there wives, just as Christ sacrificed himself for us. Nov 4, 2020

quora.com https://www.quora.com HYPERLINK "about:blank"

What are a husband's duties according to the Bible?

The main responsibility of the man is summed up in three words: "Love your wives" (Ephesians 5:25). Husbands hold the key to a flourishing marriage. Men are to be initiators. The wife comes into full fruition and submission in response to the husband loving her as he should.

harvest.org https://harvest.org

1 Peter 3:7 says, " Husbands, in the same way, be considerate as you live with your wives, and treat them with respect as the weaker partner and as heirs with you of the gracious gift of life, so that nothing will hinder your prayers."

What is the definition of a husband in the Bible?

Simply put, a husband is a man who is tasked with the roles of being a provider, Spiritual leader, and head of his household for his wife. He uses the example and inspiration of Jesus Christ to place the needs of his wife above his own in providing for her physical, emotional and Spiritual needs.

How should a godly husband treat his wife?

Treat her like the gift from God as she is. God gave to each man the woman where he was lacking, to be united as one and to care for each other's needs, accepting each other's strengths and weaknesses. a husband and wife are one body. He must honor and treat her as if it where his own body. Nov 4, 2023

How is a husband supposed to treat his wife in Christianity? - Quora quora.com https://www.quora.com HYPERLINK "about:blank"

What does the Bible say about a man belittling his wife? (NOW THIS IS A BIG ONE)

When Paul says, "husbands love your wives as Christ loved the Church" (Ephesians 5:25), he is categorically prohibiting every attitude or behavior that results in a husband devaluing, humiliating, belittling, or emotionally or physically wounding his wife.

What the Bible says about domestic violence - SAFER saferresource.org.au

Ladies don't think you're off the hook let's get to you now!

Wives, submit to your husbands as to the Lord. For the husband is the head of the wife as Christ is the head of the church, his body, of which he is the Saviour.

Ephesians 5:22-33 | GOOD NEWS for Everyone! https://goodnewsuk.com

ooh that SUBMITS WORD HURTS SOME OF YOU INDEPENDENT WOMEN. Note I don't care how independent you are YOU STILL NEED A MAN PERIOD. WE MAY THINK WE CAN DO EVERYTHING BUT WE CAN'T AND WHEN SOME OF YOU WOMEN GET THAT INTO YOUR HEAD YOU WILL NOT BE LIVING ALONE ANYMORE. MONEY IS NOT POWER; WOMEN IS NOT POWER. MEN ARE OF POWER THEY ARE OUR LEADERS FOR A REASON NOT A SEASON. FOREVER SINCE THE BEGINNING OF TIME AND NO AMOUNT OF MONEY YOU MAKE OR POSISTION YOU HOLD WILL NEVER REPLACE MAN. THAT'S THE LAW OF THE LAND PERIOD.

How should a wife treat her husband biblically?

Love your husband.
Titus 2:4 calls for wives "to love their husbands." A good description of the kind of love your husband needs is "unconditional acceptance." In other words, accept your husband just as he is—an imperfect person. Love also means being committed to a mutually fulfilling sexual relationship.

Which Bible verse says a woman should respect her husband?

Ephesians 5:33: However, each one of you also must love his wife as he loves himself, and the wife must respect her husband. Jul 24, 2023

https://www.southernliving.com HYPERLINK "about:blank" ›

How to respect your husband according to the Bible?

Respect is an action done out of obedience to the Lord.

- Watch what you say.

- Let him know when he has done something well.

- Say "Thank you".

- Recognize that he isn't perfect.

- Watch your non-verbal language.

- Seek to understand.

- Be trustworthy.

- Pray for your husband.

- Have a gentle spirit.

Https://www.radiantmarriage.com HYPERLINK "about:blank" ›

What are the duties of a wife according to the Bible?

A Wife's Role Is to Help Her Husband
God created a wife to help her husband because he was designed to need help. Men need to submit to this God-given role and allow their wives to help them. Don't be stubborn or act so macho you don't need help (Genesis 2:20). Women need to understand the meaning behind this task. May 1, 2023

https://pastorvlad.org HYPERLINK "about:blank" ›

What does the Bible say about a wife denying her husband?

Do not deprive each other except by mutual consent and for a time, so that you may devote yourselves to prayer. Then come together again so that Satan will not tempt you because of your lack of self-control. I say this as a concession, not as a command. I wish that all men were as I am.

The wife's body does not belong to her alone but also to her husband. In the same way, the husband's body does not belong to him alone but also to his wife. Do not deprive each other except by mutual consent and for a time, so that you may devote yourselves to prayer. <u>Bible Gateway 1 Corinthians 7 :: NIV - MIT</u>

What does God say about a bad wife?

23A bad wife will make her husband gloomy and depressed and break his heart. Show me a timid man who can never make up his mind, and I will show you a wife who doesn't make her husband happy. 24Sin began with a woman, and we must all die because of her.

What God says about angry wife?

Specifically Proverbs 21:9 — 'Better to live on a corner of the roof than share a house with a quarrelsome wife. ' And Proverbs 21:19 — 'Better to live in a desert than with a quarrelsome and nagging wife.

What does the Bible say about a troublesome wife?

Proverbs 27:15-16 New International Version (NIV)

A quarrelsome wife is like the dripping of a leaky roof in a rainstorm; restraining her is like restraining the wind or grasping oil with the hand.

How do I deal with a bad temper wife?

So, here are some down-to-earth tips on how to calm down your angry wife and create a happier, more peaceful home.

- Stay Calm and Collected....

- Listen, Really Listen....

- Choose Your Battles....

- Express Empathy....

- Give Her Space When Needed....

- Show Affection....

- Learn to Apologize Sincerely....

- Find the Right Time to Talk.

Sep 27, 2023

What does the Bible say about a foolish woman?

Proverbs 14:1 – "The wise woman builds her house, but the foolish pulls it down with her hands."

What God says about a good wife?

A truly good wife is the most precious treasure a man can find! Her husband depends on her, and she never lets him down. She is good to him every day of her life, and with her own hands she gladly makes clothes. She is like a sailing ship that brings food from across the sea.

Proverbs 31:10-31 CEV - Bible.com

bible.com

https://www.bible.com HYPERLINK "about:blank" › bible › PRO.31.10-31.C

What is God's punishment for adultery?

The basis for punishment of stoning specifically for adultery is clearly provided in Leviticus (20:10-12) which reads: "If a man commits adultery with another man's wife, even with the wife of his neighbor, both the adulterer and adulteress must be put to death "

Just don't give my dick away because I am going to stone you LOL just kidding that was in the past days. Now days they don't stone they do eye for an eye you do it I do it. But that don't make it right. If you don't want me just to let me, go.

Understand women we hold the key make yourself irreplaceable not too many can fit your shoes Cinderella and many not going to put up with what you have from your husband or wife. We are two different people trying to live in unity.

HAPPY WIFE HAPPY LIFE!

TILL DEATH DO US PART

Well let's start here in the Bible Proverbs 18:22 (KJV) Whoso findeth a wife findeth a good thing, and obtaineth favour of the LORD.

Numbers 30:6 (KJV) And if she had at all an husband, when she vowed, or uttered ought out of her lips, wherewith she bound her soul; What are the simplest wedding vows?

I, (NAME), take you, (NAME), to be my wedded spouse, and to live together in marriage. I promise to love you, comfort you, honor and keep you for better or worse, for richer or poorer, in sickness and health, and forsaking all others, be faithful only to you, so long as we both shall live. Mar 26, 2023

Where in the Bible is the wedding vows?

While the Bible includes verses on love, marriage, and weddings, there aren't any specific marriage vows mentioned. You can, however, use the Bible's inspirational verses in your marriage vows, include them as ceremony readings, or use a short verse as a theme on your invitations and programs. Jul 18, 2023 https://www.brides.com/ marriage-vows-in-the-bible-

5090423#:~:text=While%20the%20Bible%20includes%20 verses,on%20your%20invitations%20 and%20programs.

What does the Bible say about marital vows? Technically, nothing— there are no wedding vows for him or her in the Bible, and the Bible does not actually mention vows being required or expected in a marriage. Jul 6, 2023 https://www.marriage.com/ advice/vows/marriage-vows-in-the-bible/#:~:text=What%20 does%20the%20Bible%20say,or%20expected%20in%20 a%20marriage.

So, if there are no rules in the Bible about marital vows no wonder why people don't follow them. Its manmade, it's not written in stone so to speak. Here I was thinking I was doing what the Bible said for me to do no wonder why people find it so easy to break them. Therefore, I think that they don't care as much to marry and divorce. So, lets break this down these manmade vows.

- I take you to be my wedded spouse, and to live together in marriage. Real life I take you to be my spouse until I find someone better that will put up with my bull shit and live with you as long as we can tolerate each other so I can have a roof over my head.

- I promise to love you. Real life I promise to love you if the lust remains fun, and you can still get it up, or until the next best thing comes along and fulfill my fetuses and twisted sex styles.

- Comfort you. Real life I will be there until I don't want to hear your bull shit anymore the woes is me; I don't care anymore what you need mentally I am over it.

- Honor. Real life if I don't get caught you will be honored what you don't know want to hurt you, otherwise oops you found out so now your embarrassed, but I still did what I did can't take it back they will forget, and you will get over it until I decide to do it again.

- Keep you for better or worse. Real life in real life we have worse than better it's if I value you enough to stick it out with you or not. When it's better I have no complaints, so I am happy for now.

- For richer or poorer. Real life nothing from nothing leaves nothing so the song says Billy Preston. Richer who don't want to live a life where they can go shopping and have the finer things in life. But that takes hard work and sacrifice. at least someone must work cause if no one's working, we are poor with nothing not even hope. Riches comes easily for some marry into someone who has money, or someone who worked hard to get what they have, and the other party is given the blessing of enjoying what someone else made happen. Mind you nothing wrong with that at all. But when the poorer part comes into play many runs to the next richer and not want to stay for the poor day. Not caring that if they made it from nothing before, they could do it again with help and love. But now days it's too easy to walk away and get the next money bags. Don't get me wrong some stay and thug it out and fight together and make it work because genuine love is there.

- In sickness and health. Real life many have stayed more then leave when someone is sick, but the question is when someone is sick and not able to fulfill the personal needs of other do you thug it out or find someone else to fulfil that missing desire. Some do both have their cake and eat it too. They may stay but get that side piece male or female no bias. They both do it. Or some leave when you get sick for whatever the reason may be. Some can't handle when you're sick, they only want to be around when your healthy to be able to do things go places, don't no one want to play nurse. Or they still doing they think waiting for you to die so they can get some of your money and move on to the next. I have watched people when their spouse passed away the next week, they had someone else. Most of the time they already had someone in waiting. Now some will thug it out because they really do love their spouse and being without them is worse than death itself. That the Agape love real love the love that God put together and that is till death do us part.

- Forsaking all others. Real life most of the time you always have someone who don't want you married. Friend, family Mother's in laws from hell. I had the mother-in-law from hell she didn't want me married to her son no matter how good I was to him. That a whole new book to write. And my husband wanted to appease his mother, so I got screwed over on that part. I came last most of the time in our younger years until he realized that she wasn't going to change. Some people forget that your spouse comes first then everyone else. Let me say that again spouse comes first. I say mother in laws because they are the most major part of marriages failing when it comes to this part of the vows.

- Be faithful only to you, so long as we both shall live. This the big one. Real life. Being faithful now days is rare. The myth that we don't have enough men to go around is bull shit. Are there enough women for every man?

It's very unlikely that there are exactly as much women as there are men. Whether there are more men or women is unknown. But not everyone wants to be in a relationship, and not everyone wants to be in a relationship with someone of the opposite gender. Dec 28, 2018 https://www.quora.com/Are-there-enough-women-in-the- world-to-match-with-every-man#:~:text=It HYPERLINK "https:// www.quora.com/Are-there-enough-women-in-the-world-to-match- with-every-man#:~:text=It's%20very%20 unlikely%20that%20 there,someone%20of%20the%20 opposite%20gender"' HYPERLINK "https://www.quora. com/Are-there-enough-women-in-the-world-to- match-with-every-man#:~:text=It's%20very%20unlikely%20that%20 there,someone%20of%20the%20opposite%20gender"s%20 very%20 unlikely%20that%20there,someone%20of%20 the%20opposite%20 gender. Is there really a man for every woman?

Is there a man for every woman? The idea that there is a perfect match for every person is a romantic notion, but it's not necessarily a universal truth. While some people may find a lifelong partner who feels like the perfect match for them, others may not. So being faithful for the rest of your life is very hard some do it most don't. Nor do they try for many reasons the devil's playground since Sodom and Gomorrah women have been the death of men. They can't live without it. Fake or real they must stick something or someone. Women pussy controls the world rather you believe it or not. But its up to you to do right by your spouse. Pussy is pussy all do the same thing just a different person. Although they all don't look the same cause some of you women have been ran through you have some ugly kitties. That only a man can love. And some women!

Some people do believe in till death do us part like a form of ownership. Where they mentally want to control a person and will even kill for that person, kill themselves, or the person they love so much because they rather them be gone so no one else can have them then to let them go. That is no longer love that is a sickness and obsession that needs to get some help with. You shouldn't love someone that much that you would take their and your life for. You can find a new love.

Story time!!!! Since where on the line of killing people for the sake of love. No, I wasn't obsessed with trying to kill for love but because of the disrespect and lies, and what I call the Judas kiss. I was fed up with the women and the friend he fucked with in my face I was going to kill this bitch for real and till this day God have kept me away from that ugly nasty ass whore bitch. Now in the beginning of the book I told you that one woman didn't know how close she was to being killed. So let me tell you to remind you how deep things can get. But in the end, I choose me. For the first time I understood how people could make people snap. I was almost there. God knows I was there. I scared myself if it wasn't for the love of my children and my belief in God that bitch would be dead, and I would have been in jail or gotten away with it. The plan was to get away with it. You never know which way it would have gone but a life would have been lost all because I let my emotions get the best of me.

So anyway, one day my husband was over to his brother's house and as I walked up to the door, I had a chill all through my body it stopped me before I walked in. so, I asked God what's going on and he just said watch out for her. So, I said OKAY not knowing what I was going to walk into I just braced myself. So, I walked in and saw my husband and this whore and my brother in-law and his girlfriend at the time playing dominos they were key keying and just having a good time until I walked in so I told him lets go home what was he doing no one said nothing then I looked at this ugly as bitch and I knew that God was talking about her.

Sure, enough she would end up having sex with my husband an affair as you will say. Fast forward. I guess she started thinking that she was going to get him whenever she wanted. Mind you we all party together did each other hair watched each other kids they called me auntie. But she had no loyalty to me for she was my brother-in-law girlfriend best friend and his cousin boyfriend's sister. Anyway, so come to find out he had been going to a reggae club with them left me at home with the kids and I never even knew he was going. I thought he was at family house. So, they had been messing around for a while at this point. So, one day guess he wasn't accessible to her anymore when she wanted him. See with my husband when he done, or he feels like you're doing too much, and I will find out he try to cut it off. But she didn't want to cut it off she like the dick.

Mind you she had her own man that was living out of state coming back and forth. So, on face book they decided to start giving me hints and wanted it to be known that they were fucking so they sent me a picture for her twerking on his dick and how they were just getting it in. So I went to her and asked her was she fucking my husband and showed her the picture. She said they was just dancing and drunk I said you don't dance that close to no one's man or husband what would she think if I was doing her husband that way. She said you right I am sorry I being gullible I guess you would say believe her or at least I wanted to think it wasn't so.

I said that you should take that down cause if I think something is going on your man will too if he sees it. And I still was trying to protect my husband because I didn't want him to end up fighting with her man. So, in that same day she gave me a hug real tight and said Lavetta I wouldn't never do you like that first he too old for me. I guess he was about 8 years older than her and him just like a brother to me nothing more. And I know you really love him grab me and hug me real tight whisper in my ear and said I love you and gave me a kiss on my right cheek what I call the Judas kiss. So that day I left, and she said she would have them take it down that she didn't know who did it. But they were all in it together.

Fast forward Valentine's Day they all rented a hotel room, and I don't know if they were going to have an orgy or what, but it was 6 in one room on Valentine's Day. So, they were blowing his cell phone up and then I ask what going on you are going somewhere, and he said no I am here with you I said why they keep calling you he said he didn't know. So, they were mad that he didn't show up so on Valentine's Day they sent me another Facebook message this time titled "YOUR HUSBAND FUCKING' and then when I opened it up, they told who and how long. Give real name. I showed him and put him out that day. And never celebrated valentines again since.

So not sure when I really snapped but I started getting sick and every time I went to the hospital, I would steal me a scapple. See I was a going to be a good killer. I didn't want to shoot you too messy, I didn't want to stab her too much work, so if I had a scapple, I could just slice her and go, and she wouldn't know what hit her. That was my theory of it all. It was set that how I was going to kill her.

I would follow her I knew where she lived, I would watch her, and she didn't even know it. But my family found out that I had them. So, they would hide them from me my husband was back home, but he knew I had them and would also hide them from me thinking I was going to use them on him. Some would say blame him not her. But I blamed them both. Her first. Cause she gave me the Judas kiss. And lied to my face and was and I called her friend at this point I was fed up with him messing around on me with people I knew that was close to me that I thought was my friend. I had kids by him 7 of them that was my kids' father, so I wasn't going to hurt my kids that way.

Every time they hid my scapple, I would get some more. I would keep them in my purse for the right moment. But I stopped after a couple of years I started thinking that she wasn't worth it. What if I got caught and I go to jail I not only lose my life I wouldn't see or be with my kids and grand kids again and he would still be free to get another woman. So why do it. So, five years pass but I couldn't get over this last escapade, so I filed for a divorce. I was done. That was it. I wanted to get out. No more I had enough, and it kept playing in my mind even if he wasn't seeing her anymore. Funny part his mother called her family and would till this day party with her and call her family she partied with most of the women he messed with because she was happy that it was anyone besides me.

I am so happy that God loved me so not to allow me to lose my life over people who didn't give one fuck well they did fuck but just had no respect for me or love at that point. But I loved me and my kids more to not give into my second of emotion that would have destroyed my life forever. THANK YOU, JESUS!

SO, I BEG YOU TO GET HELP PRAY AND LOVE YOUR SELF MORE BEFORE YOU GIVE INTO AN EMOTION THAT CAN CHANGE YOUR LIFE WORSER THEN SOMEONE WHO DIDN'T HAVE LOVE FOR THEMSELVES OR RESPECT. KARMA IS REAL AND ONE DAY SOMEONE WILL RETURN WHAT WAS DONE TO ME. AND I FOR GIVE HER NOT FOR HER BUT FOR MYSELF. MY LIFE HAS NOT STOPPED AND I AM ABLE TO LIVE ANOTHER DAY WITH MY FAMILY. THAT IS WORTH EVERYTHING. I TRADED MY LIFE

FOR THEIRS. BECAUSE I COULDN'T DO THAT TO THEM. I COULDN'T TAKE THEIR MOTHER AWAY IT WOULDN'T BE FAIR TO THEM WHEN ALL I HAD TO DO IS GET ANOTHER MAN. ITS ONE OUT THERE FOR ME. AND THIS TIME IT WILL BE DIFFERENT. NOT PERFECT BUT DIFFERENT.

RELIGIOUS VIEW(S) ON WHAT A MARRIAGE SHOULD BE

Islamic marital practices

From Wikipedia, the free encyclopedia

<table><tr><td>

This article **needs additional citations for verification**.
Please help improve this article by adding citations to reliable sources.
Unsourced material may be challenged and removed.
Find sources: " HYPERLINK "https://www.google.com/search?as_eq=wikipedia&q=%22Islamic+marital+practices%22"Islamic marital practices HYPERLINK "https://www.google.com/search?as_eq=wikipedia&q=%22Islamic+marital+practices%22"" – news · newspapers · books · scholar · JSTOR (October 2010) (Learn how and when to remove this template message)

</td></tr></table>

A portrait of newly married Bengali Muslim couple from Dhaka, Bangladesh in 2014

A <u>Sundanese</u> wedding ceremony held inside a <u>mosque</u> in <u>West Java</u>, <u>Indonesia</u> in 1977.

The <u>Mughal Emperor</u> <u>Shah Jahan</u> attends the marriage procession of his eldest son <u>Dara Shikoh</u>. Mughal era <u>fireworks</u> were utilized to brighten the night throughout the wedding ceremony.

Muslim marriage and **Islamic wedding customs** are traditions and practices that relate to <u>wedding</u> ceremonies and <u>marriage</u> rituals prevailing within the <u>Muslim world</u>. Although Islamic marriage customs and relations vary depending on country of origin and government regulations, both Muslim men and women from around the world are guided by Islamic laws and practices specified in the Quran.[1] Islamic marital jurisprudence allows Muslim men to be married to multiple women (a practice known as <u>polygyny</u>).

According to the teachings of the <u>Quran</u>, a married Muslim couple is equated with clothing. Within this context, both husband and wife are each other's protector and comforter, just as real garments "show and conceal" the body of human beings. Thus, they are meant "for one another".[2] The Quran continues to discuss the matter of marriage and states, "And among His Signs is this, that he created for you mates from among yourselves, that you may dwell in tranquility with them, and He has put love and mercy between your [hearts]…".[3] Marriages within the Muslim community are incredibly important. The purpose of marriage in Islamic culture is to preserve the religion through the creation of a family. The family is meant to be "productive and constructive, helping and encouraging one another to be good and righteous, and competing with one another in good works".[4]

Choice of partner

Application of <u>Mehndi</u> or <u>Henna</u> is common for <u>Muslims</u> brides.

In Islam, <u>polygyny</u> is allowed with certain restrictions; <u>polyandry</u> is not. The Quran directly addresses the matter of polygyny in Chapter 4 Verse 3: "...Marry of the women that you please: two, three, or four. But if you feel that you should not be able to deal justly, then only one or what your right hand possesses. That would be more suitable to prevent you from doing injustice."[5] The Prophet accepts the marriage of multiple wives but only if the husband's duties will not falter as a result

Kissing is prohibited before the Nikkah and is highly disliked in public after the wedding.[6]

Although practices of polygamy have declined in practice and acceptance in most parts of the Muslim world (such as Turkey and Tunisia who have completely outlawed it), it is still legal in over 150 countries in Africa, Middle East, and most countries in the third world.[7] HYPERLINK "https://en.wikipedia.org/wiki/Islamic_ marital_practices#cite_note-8"[8] Since the 20th century and the rise of major feminist movements, polygamous marriages have severely declined. With changing economic conditions, female empowerment, and acceptance of family planning practices, polygamy seems to be severely declining as an acceptable and viable marriage practice within the Muslim world.[9]

In regards to interfaith marriages and partners, the rules for Muslim women are much more restrictive than the rules applied to Muslim men wishing to marry a non-Muslim.[10]

The specific passages of Islamic text that address the issue of interfaith marriage are in Quran 5:5, as well as in Quran 60:10:

> This day the good things are allowed to you... ; and the chaste from among the believing women and the chaste from among those who have been given the Book before you (are lawful for you); when you have given them their dowries, taking (them) in marriage, not fornicating nor taking them for paramours in secret...[10]

> O you who believe!... ; and hold not to the ties of marriage of unbelieving women, and ask for what you have spent, and let them ask for what they have spent. That is Allah's judgment; He judges between you, and Allah is Knowing, Wise.[10]

Despite the Quranic text that seem to detest interfaith marriage [*example needed*], a growing movement of modern Islamic scholars are beginning to reinterpret and reexamine traditional Shari'a interpretations. While these scholars use "established and approved methodologies" in order to claim new conclusions, they are still met with a considerable amount of opposition from the majority of orthodox Islamic scholars and interpreters.[10]

Islamic dating practices and community programs

In most Islamic societies and communities it is not a common practice for young people to actively seek a partner for themselves by following modern and Western rituals, such as dating. Young Muslim men and women are strongly encouraged to marry as soon as possible, since the family is considered the foundation of Islamic society.[1]

According to traditional Islamic law, women and men are not free to date or intermingle, which results in a more drawn-out and deliberate process.[1] The amount of choice and acceptance involved in choosing marriage partners often depends on the class and educational status of the family when it comes to society. In the religion itself though, choosing your partner is allowed and encouraged as long as there are no inappropriate relations, such as dating or being physical.[1] Some important characteristics in choosing a worthy mate are faith and chastity. These traits are pointed out in Quran Chapter 33 Verse 35 "For Muslim men and women, for believing men and women, for true men and women, for men and women who are patient and for men and women who guard their chastity, and for men and women who engage much in Allah's praise, for them has Allah prepared forgiveness and great reward."[1] 'Forced' marriages, where consent has not been given by the bride, or is given only under excessive pressure, is considered illegal in all schools of Islamic law. Forced marriage is absolutely and explicitly forbidden.

Since traditional Muslim societies are generally religiously homogeneous, it is much easier for individuals to find socially acceptable partners through traditional methods. Within these communities, families, friends, and services are used to help people find a significant other.[11] However, in non-Muslim countries, like the United States, there is no universal method for matchmaking or finding a spouse. These Muslims must use alternate methods in order to find a partner in a way that closely simulates the traditional process.

Muslims in non-Islamic countries like the United States use Islamic institutions or imams to help them find partners. Islamic institutions like the ISNA (Islamic Society of North America), NOI (Nation of Islam), ICNA (Islamic Circle of North

America), and MANA (Muslim Alliance of North America), allow individuals to meet others at annual conventions.[12] The imam is a valued source among these Muslim communities as well. For any individual who values religious piety in a partner and does not have a Muslim social network, the imam is a valuable source of guidance.

The internet also offers new opportunities for Muslim individuals to meet one another. In the past 10 years, Matchmaking sites for Muslims have become an increasingly popular way to meet one's spouse.[13] The website, SingleMuslim.com one of the first matchmaking sites is very successful. Adeem Younis, the founder of the website, designed it in accordance with Islamic principles. Halal sites like SingleMuslim.com and helahel.com ask questions about individuals' piety including prayer habits, fasting, and if they have made the hajj pilgrimage.[14] Among Islamic theological figures there is some dispute over the validity of these websites; however, these sites continue to be created and avidly used. According to Younis, "Because 'dating' is not allowed in Islam, the Internet is an ideal vehicle for a discreet first step in finding a marriage partner."[14] Websites such as, The International Muslim Matrimonial site, broaden the depth of choices for individuals looking for a partner.[15] Individual interests like, hobbies, political views, passions, activities, and family values, are all included to make a user profile. In some societies in both the Islamic world and the West, traditional matchmaking practices do not necessarily include this kind of expression of personal characteristics; therefore, these websites expand individuality while maintaining traditional Islamic ideals of matchmaking.[12]

Diversity of Muslim weddings

A Kazakh wedding ceremony in a mosque

Considering that there are over 2 billions Muslims in the Muslim World, there is no single way for all Muslim weddings to be held. There are 49 Muslim majority countries and each contains many regional and cultural differences. Additionally, many Muslims living in the West then mix family traditions with their host countries. [16]

United States

Muslims in the United States come from many backgrounds, but the largest segment are those from South Asia, Arab countries, and more recently from East Africa. When it comes to Muslim weddings the culture they come from heavily influences the kind of rituals that will take place. Similarly American-Muslims e.g. African-Americans, Caucasians, Hispanics and others have elements of both local, and Muslim influence. The central event in all American-Muslim Weddings will be the Nikah. This is the actual wedding ceremony, usually officiated by a Muslim cleric, an Imam. Although a Nikah can be done anywhere including the bride's home or reception hall, it is preferable and usually done in a mosque. [16]

A Muslim Wedding Survey of North American Muslims, revealed among other things the merger of two or more cultures. For example, the two most popular wedding dress colors are red and white. Whereas in traditional Muslim countries marriages have been arranged, in the United States, 57.75% of weddings are through friends, online or people the person has met at work. [17]

China

Muslim General <u>Ma Jiyuan</u>'s wedding with a <u>Kuomintang</u> flag in the background.

Prominent Muslims in China, such as generals, followed standard marriage practices in the 20th century, such as using western clothing like white wedding dresses.

<u>Chinese Muslim</u> marriages resemble typical Chinese marriages except traditional Chinese religious rituals are not used.[18]

Indian subcontinent

Main articles: <u>Bangladeshi wedding</u>, <u>Pakistani wedding</u>, and *<u>Indian wedding</u>*

A <u>Bangladeshi Muslim bride</u> with her family.

Muslims in the <u>Indian subcontinent</u> normally follow marriage customs that are similar to those practiced by Muslims of the <u>Middle-East</u>, which are based on Islamic convention.[19] These Islamic traditions were first handed down to <u>medieval</u> Indians by propagators of the Islamic religion that involved <u>sultans</u> and <u>Moghul</u> rulers at the time.[20] The <u>blueprint</u> is the same as the Middle-Eastern *Nikah*,[19] a pattern seen in marriage ceremonies of <u>Sunnis</u> and <u>Shias</u>.[20] Traditional Muslim Indian wedding celebrations typically last for three days.[19] Prior to the observance of the wedding ceremony proper, two separate pre-wedding rituals, which involve traditional dancing and singing, occurs in two places: at the groom's house and at the bride's home.[20]

On the eve of the wedding day, a bridal service known as the *Mehndi* ritual or henna ceremony is held at the bride's home. This ritual is sometimes done two days before the actual wedding day. During this bridal preparation ritual, turmeric paste is placed on the bride's skin for the purpose of improving and brightening her complexion, after which mehndi is applied on the bride's hands and feet by the *mehndiwali*, a female relative. [19] HYPERLINK "https://en.wikipedia. org/wiki/Islamic_marital_practices#cite_note-ZawajIndian-20"[20]

Now long abandoned, anointing the teeth with a powder called 'missī' in order to blacken them used to be part of Islamic wedding rituals in India.[21]

The Indian Islamic wedding ceremony is also preceded by a marriage procession known as the groom's *baraat*. From this convoy arrives the groom, who will share a sherbet drink with a brother of his bride at the place of the marriage ceremony. This drinking ritual happens as the sisters of the bride engage in tomfooleries and playfully strike guests using flower-filled cudgels.[19]

The wedding ceremony, known as *Nikah*,[22] is officiated by the *Maulvi*, a priest also called *Qazi*.[19] HYPERLINK "https://en.wikipedia.org/wiki/Islamic_marital_practices#cite_note-ZawajIndian-20"[20] Among the important wedding participants are the *Walises*, or the fathers of both groom and bride.[19] and the bride's legal representative.[20] It is the bride's father who promises his daughter's hand to the groom, a ritual known as the *Kanya-dhan*.[20] Also in this formal occasion, particularly in conventional Islamic weddings, when men and women typically have separate seating arrangements. Another common practice are wedding sequences that include the reading of Quranic verses, the groom's proposal and bride's acceptance parts known as the *Ijab-e-Qubul*[19] or the *ijab* and *qabul*;[20] the decision-making of the bride's and groom's families regarding the price of the matrimonial financial endowment known as the *Mehar* HYPERLINK "https://en.wikipedia.org/wiki/Islamic_marital_practices#cite_note-Zawaj3days-19"[19] or *Mehr* (a dower no less than ten dirhams HYPERLINK "https://en.wikipedia.org/wiki/Islamic_marital_practices#cite_note-ZawajIndian-20"[20]), which will come from the family of bridegroom. Blessings and prayers are then given by older women and other guests to the couple.[19] In return the groom gives salutatory *salaam* wishes to his blessers, especially to female elders.[20] The bride also usually receives gifts known generally as the *burri*, which may be in the form of gold jewelries, garments, money, and the like.[20]

The marriage contract is known as the *Nikaahnama*, and is signed not only by the couple but also by the Walises and the Maulvi.[19]

After the Nikah, the now married couple joins each other to be seated among gender-segregated attendees.[19] The groom is customarily brought first to the women's area in order for him to be able to present gifts to his wife's sister.[20] Although jointly seated, the bride and the groom can only observe one another via mirrors, and a copy of the Quran is placed in between their assigned seats. With their heads sheltered by a *dupatta* and while guided by the Maulvi, the couple reads Muslim prayers.[19]

After the wedding ceremony, the bride is brought to the house of her husband, where she is welcomed by her mother-in-law, who holds a copy of the Quran over her head.[19]

The wedding reception hosted by the groom family is known as the *Valimah*[19] or the *Dawat-e-walima*.[20]

As per Muslim Personal Law Sharia Application Act of 1937, which is applicable to all Muslims in India (except in the state of Goa), polygamy is legal: a Muslim man may marry a maximum of four women without divorce and with few conditions. Following are the laws applicable to Muslims in India (except in the state of Goa) regarding matters of marriage, succession, Inheritance etc.

- Muslim Personal Law Sharia Application Act,1937

- The Dissolution Of Muslim Marriages Act, 1939

- Muslim Women's Protection of Rights on Divorce Act,1986

Note: Above laws are not applicable in the state of Goa, as state of Goa has Uniform Civil Code i.e. same law irrespective of religion, caste or nationality.

The Malay Archipelago

A <u>Minangkabau</u> wedding ceremony in <u>Indonesia</u>. In a traditional Minangkabau wedding, the bride and groom will sit together in a traditional wedding lounge known as the *pelaminan* throughout the celebration.

<u>Malay</u> wedding traditions (<u>Malay</u>: *Adat Perkahwinan Melayu*; <u>Jawi</u> <u>script</u>: عادة ڤرکهوينن نملايي و), such as those that occur in <u>Brunei</u>, <u>Singapore</u>, <u>Malaysia</u>, and parts of <u>Indonesia</u> and <u>Thailand</u>, normally include the *lamaran* or <u>marriage</u> <u>proposal</u>, the <u>betrothal</u>, the determination of the bridal dowry known as the *hantaran* agreed upon by both the parents' of the groom and the bride (usually done one year before the solemnization of marriage), delivery of gifts and the dowry (*istiadat hantar belanja*), the marriage solemnization (*upacara akad nikah*) at

the bride's home or in a <u>mosque</u>, the henna application ritual known as the *berinai*, the <u>costume</u> changing of the couple known as the *tukar pakaian* for <u>photography</u> sessions, followed by <u>wedding reception</u>, a feast-meal for guests (*pesta pernikahan* or *resepsi pernikahan or kenduri kahwin*) usually took place in the weekend (Saturday or Sunday), and the *bersanding* or the sitting-in-state ceremony when the couple sit in elaborate *pelaminan* (wedding throne) at their own home, or in <u>wedding hall</u> during the wedding reception.[23]

Prior to being able to meet his bride, sometimes a *mak andam*, a "<u>beautician</u>", or any member of the family of the bride will intercept the groom to delay the joining of the would-be spouses; only after the groom was able to pay a satisfactory "entrance fee" could he finally meet his bride. The wedding ceremony proper is usually held on a weekend, and involves exchanging of gifts, Quranic readings and recitation, and displaying of the couple while within a bridal chamber. While seated at their *pelaminan* "wedding throne", the newly-weds are showered with uncooked rice and petals, objects that signify <u>fertility</u>. The guests of the wedding celebration are typically provided by the couple with gifts known as the *bunga telur* ("egg flower") or bunga pahar (egg branches). The gifted eggs are traditionally eggs dyed with red coloring and are placed inside cups or other suitable containers bottomed with <u>glutinous rice</u>. These eggs also symbolize fertility, a marital wish hoping that the couple will bear many offspring. However, these traditional gifts are now sometimes replaced by non-traditional chocolates, jellies, or soaps. [24] The guest will be served with various kinds of foods, depends on the local traditions.

The marriage contract that binds the marital union is called the *Akad Nikah*, a verbal agreement sealed by a financial sum known as the *mas kahwin*, and witnessed by three persons.

Unlike in the past when the father of the bride customarily acts as the <u>officiant</u> for the ceremonial union, current-day Muslim weddings are now officiated by the *kadhi*, a marriage official and <u>Shariat (or) Syariah</u> Court religious officer.[24] In Indonesia Muslim weddings are officiated and led by the *penghulu*, the official of *Kantor Urusan Agama* (KUA or Office of Religious Affairs). The *Akad Nikah* might be performed in the Office of Religious Affairs, or the *penghulu* is invited to a ceremonial place outside the Religious Affair Office (mosque, bride's house or <u>wedding hall</u>).[25]

The Philippines

<u>Muslim communities</u> in the <u>Philippines</u> include the <u>Tausug</u> and T'boli tribe, a group of people in <u>Jolo</u>, Sulu who practice matrimonial activities based on their own ethnic legislation and the laws of Islam. Their customary and legal matrimony is composed of negotiated <u>arranged marriage</u> (*pagpangasawa*), marriage through the "<u>game</u> of <u>abduction</u>" (*pagsaggau*), and <u>elopement</u> (*pagdakup*).[26] Furthermore, although Tausug men may acquire two wives, bigamous or plural marriages are rare.[26]

A *<u>Filipino Tausug</u>* lady performing the traditional *<u>pangalay</u>* dance.

Tausug matrimonial customs generally include the negotiation and proclamation of the *bridewealth* (the *ungsud*) which is a composition of the "valuables for the offspring" or *dalaham pagapusan* (in the form of money or an animal that cannot be slaughtered for the marital feast); the "valuables dropped in the ocean" or *dalaham hug a tawid*, which are intended for the father of the bride; the *basingan* which is a payment – in the form of antique gold or silver Spanish or American coins – for the transference of kingship rights toward the *usba* or "male side"; the "payment to the treasury" (*sikawin baytal- mal*, a payment to officers of the law and wedding officiants); the wedding musicians and performers; wedding feast costs; and the guiding proverb that says a lad should marry by the time he has already personally farmed for a period of three years. This is the reason why young Tausug males and females typically marry a few years after they reached the stage of puberty.[27]

Regular arranged Islamic marriages through negotiation are typically according to parental wishes, although sometimes the son will also suggest a woman of his choice. This is the ideal, esteemed, and considered "most proper" in the legal point of view of Tausug culture, despite of being a time-consuming and costly practice for the groom. If the parents disagree with their son's choice of a woman to marry, he might decide to resort to a marriage by abducting the woman of his choice, run away, run amuck, or choose to become an outlaw. In relation to this type of marriage, another trait that is considered ideal in Tausug marriage is to wed sons and daughters with first or second cousins, due to the absence of difficulty in negotiating and simplification of land inheritance discussions.[26] However, there is also another way of arranging a Tausug marriage, which is through the establishment of *maglillah pa maas sing babai* or by "surrendering to the lady's parents", wherein the lad proclaims his intention while at the house of the parents of the woman of his choice; he will not depart until he receives permission to marry. In other circumstances, the lad offers a sum of money to the parents of the lass; a refusal by the father and mother of the woman would mean paying a fine or doubling the price offered by the negotiating man.[27] "Abduction-game marriages" are characteristically in accord with the grooms' requests, and are performed either by force or "legal fiction". [26] This strategy of marrying a woman is actually a "*courtship* game" that expresses a Tausug man's masculinity and bravery. Although the woman has the right to refuse marrying her "abductor", reluctance and refusal does not always endure because the man will resort to seducing the "abductee". In the case of marriages done through the game of abduction, the bridewealth offered is a gesticulation to appease the woman's parents.[26]

Elopements are normally based on the brides' desires, which may, at times, are made to resemble a "bride kidnapping" situation (i.e. a marriage through the game of abduction) in order to prevent dishonoring the woman who wished to be eloped.[26] One way of eloping is known to the Tausugs as *muuy magbana* or the "homecoming to get hold of a husband", wherein a Tausug woman offers herself to the man of her choice or to the parents of the man who she wants to become her spouse. Elopement is also a strategy used by female Tausugs in order to be able to enter into a second marriage, or done by an older unwed lady by seducing a man who is younger than her.[28]

During the <u>engagement</u> period, the man may render service to his bride's parents in the form of performing household chores. [29] After the period of engagement has lapsed, the marital-union ceremony is observed by feastings, delivery of the whole bridewealth, slaughtering of a <u>carabao</u> or a <u>cow</u>, playing <u>gongs</u> and native <u>xylophones</u>, reciting prayers in the <u>Arabic</u> and <u>Tausug languages</u>, symbolic touching by the groom of his bride's forehead, and the couple's emotionless sitting-together ritual. In some instances when a groom is marrying a young bride, the engagement period may last longer until the Tausug lass has reached the right age to marry; or the matrimonial ceremony may proceed – a wedding the Tausug termed as "to marry in a handkerchief" or *kawin ha saputangan* – because the newly-wed man can live after marriage at the home of his parents-in-law but cannot have marital sex with his wife until she reaches the legal age.[29]

Tausug culture also allows the practice of divorce.[29]

There are also other <u>courtship</u>, <u>marriage</u>, and <u>wedding customs</u> in the Philippines.

United Arab Emirates

Main article: <u>Arab wedding</u>

A bride's hand decorated with <u>henna</u>.

Generally, wedding ceremonies in the <u>United Arab Emirates</u> traditionally involves scheduling the wedding date, preparation for the bride and groom, and carousing with dancing and singing which takes place one week or less prior to the wedding night. Bridal preparation is done by women by anointing the body of the bride with oil, application of perfumes to the bride's hair, use of creams, feeding the bride with special dishes, washing the bride's hair with amber and jasmine extracts, use of the <u>Arabian Kohl</u> or Arabian <u>eye</u> <u>liner</u>, and decorating the hands and feet with henna (a ritual known as the *Laylat Al Henna* or "henna night" or "night of henna", and performed a few days before being wed; during this evening, other members of the bride's family and guests also place henna over their own hands). The Emirati bride stays at her dwelling for forty days until the marriage night, only to be visited by her family. Later, the groom offers her items that she will use to create the *Addahbia*, a dowry which is composed of jewelry, perfumes, and silk, among others.[30] [*unreliable source?*]

In <u>Dubai</u>, one of <u>the seven emirates</u> of the <u>UAE</u>, the traditional <u>Bedouin</u> wedding is a ceremonial that echoes the earliest Arab concept of <u>matrimony</u>, which emphasizes that marital union is not simply a joining of a man and a woman but the coming together of two families. Traditionally lasting for seven days, Bedouin marriage preparations and celebration starts with the marriage proposal known as the *Al Khoutha*, a meeting of the groom's father and bride's father; the purpose of the groom's father is to ask the hand of the bride from the bride's father for marriage; and involves the customary drinking of minty Arab tea. After this, the negotiating families proceed with the *Al Akhd*, a marriage contract agreement. The bride goes through the ritual of a "bridal shower" known as *Laylat Al Henna*, the henna tattooing of the bride's hands and feet, a service signifying attractiveness, fortune, and healthiness. The *Al Aadaa* follows, a groom-teasing rite done by the friends of the bride wherein they ask compensation after embellishing the bride with henna. The ceremonial also involves a family procession towards the bride's home, a re-enactment of a war dance known as *Al Ardha*, and the *Zaahbaah* or the displaying of the bride's garments and the gifts she received from her groom's family. In the earliest versions of Bedouin wedding ceremonies, the groom and the bride goes and stays within a tent made of camel hair, and that the bride is not to be viewed in public during the nuptial proceedings. The wedding concludes with the *Tarwaah*, when the bride rides a camel towards her new home to live with her husband. After a week, the bride will have a reunion with her own family. Customarily, the groom will not be able to join his bride until the formal wedding procedure ended. The only place where they will finally see each other is at their post-wedding dwelling.[31] Established Bedouin wedding customs also entail the use of hand- embroidered costumes, the dowry, and the bridewealth. Islamic law dictates that the jewelry received by the bride becomes her personal property.[31][*unreliable source*]

Islamic marriage contract

From Wikipedia, the free encyclopedia

An 1874 Islamic marriage contract.

A bride signing the *nikah nama* (marriage contract).

An **Islamic marriage contract** is considered an integral part of an Islamic marriage, and outlines the rights and responsibilities of the groom and bride or other parties involved in marriage proceedings under Sharia. Whether it is considered a formal, binding contract depends on the jurisdiction. Islamic faith marriage contracts are not valid in English law.[1]

Witnessing

In Sunni Islam, a marriage contract must have at least two witnesses. Proper witnessing is critical to the validation of the marriage, also acting as a protection against suspicions of adulterous relationships.

In Shia Islam, witnesses to a marriage are not necessary.[2] It is also believed that temporary marriage, or Nikah Mut HYPERLINK "https://en.wikipedia.org/wiki/Nikah_Mut%27ah"' HYPERLINK "https://en.wikipedia.org/wiki/Nikah_Mut%27ah"ah (a type of contract which had more relaxed requirements) was prohibited in Sunni Islam, the necessity of witnessing was introduced by Sunni caliphs, specifically Umar, to ensure that no couples engaged in secret union.

Authorization

Marriages are usually not held in <u>mosques</u>, (depending on the country and culture of both where the marriage happens and the parties involved) because typically men and women are separated during the ceremony and reception. In <u>Sunni</u> Islam, there is no official clergy, so any Muslim who understands the Islamic tradition can be the official for the wedding. However, if a Muslim wedding is held in a mosque, then a <u>marriage officiant</u>, known as *qadi*, *qazi* or *madhun* (<u>Arabic</u>: مأذون), may preside over the wedding.[3]

Contract

The <u>rights of women</u> proceeding the <u>Advent of Islam</u> HYPERLINK "https://en.wikipedia.org/wiki/Islamic_marriage_contract#cite_ note-4"[4] as changed drastically to where they stand in society in the twenty first century. Prior to the Advent of Islam, men were allowed to marry or divorce whenever they pleased leading to a number of problems within the society. The current status of marriage in Islam, however, is seen at equal and fair to both men and women and signals the start of family.

The <u>Quran</u> states that you should love your husband or wife, however, <u>divorce</u> is not forbidden. The lifestyles men and women go through following a divorce are very different, women must participate in a period of abstinence and remain single for a period of time.[5] This period of abstinence and being single allows for the father, if the wife was pregnant before the divorce, to know if the unborn child belongs to them or not.[5]

Among the stipulations that can be included in the marriage contract include giving up, or demanding, certain responsibilities.

[6] The contract may also be used to regulate the couple's physical relationship, if needed. [*citation needed*]

The marriage contract can also specify where the couple will live, whether or not the first wife will allow the husband to take a second wife without her consent. The wife has the right to initiate divorce, it is called khula. She either gives back the dowry (mahr) or does not, depending on the reason for divorce. The man has the right to divorce. The marriage contract somewhat resembles the marriage settlements once negotiated for upper-class Western brides, but can extend to non-financial matters usually ignored by marriage settlements or pre-nuptial agreements.

Purposes

One important purpose of the contract is to make sexual intercourse legal. This is supported by various Hadiths and quotations:

Sahih Bukhari, Book 62, #81:[7] HYPERLINK "https://en.wikipedia. org/wiki/Islamic_marriage_contract#cite_note-8"[8]

- *Narrated 'Uqba: The Prophet (peace and blessings of Allah be upon him) said: "The stipulations [in the marriage contract] most entitled to be abided by are those with which you are given the right to enjoy the (women's) private parts."*

Al-Mughni (by Ibn Qudaamah), Kitab al Nikah:[9]

- *... the Prophet (peace and blessings of Allah be upon him) [said]: "The most deserving of conditions to be fulfilled* *are those by means of which sexual intercourse becomes permissible for you."*

Cited in (Al Aqad, 2014) the common problem of translation of marriage contracts is due to the varieties of word synonyms in the legal Arabic system which have no equivalence in the English system in terms of marriage contracts, such as: مهر, شبكه, صداق - Mahr, Shabkah, Sadaq- (dowry), whereas, all of these examples attributed and affected by the culture and tradition of the Arabic language.[10]

Interfaith Marriage

<u>Interfaith marriage</u> has been a growing concept in the past few years but according to the Quran, Muslims should only marry other Muslims and without doing so can lead to problems within and outside of the families.

One main problem with interfaith marriage as seen in the Islamic community is the fear that one might abandon their faith or their children will not grow up in it.[11] Another issue that can arise is the conflict directly between the two married individuals if their religious traditions get in the way of the other, leading to a debate of which religion should be the more prominent one in the relationship.

Jewish views on marriage

From Wikipedia, the free encyclopedia

This article **needs additional citations for verification**. Please help improve this article by adding citations to reliable sources. Unsourced material may be challenged and removed.
Find sources: " HYPERLINK "https:// www.google.com/search?as_ eq=wikipedia&q=%22Jewish+views+on+marriage%22"Jewish views on marriage HYPERLINK "https://www.google.com/search?as_ eq=wikipedia&q=%22Jewish+views+on+marriage%22""
– news · newspapers · books · scholar · JSTOR (August 2022) (*Learn how and when to remove this template message*)

A Jewish wedding (1903) by Jozef Israëls

Jewish marriage certificate, dated 1740 (Brooklyn Museum)

The Jewish Bride (Rembrandt, 1662–6)

Marriage in Judaism is the documentation of a contract between a Jewish man and a Jewish woman in which God is involved. In Judaism, a marriage can end either because of a divorce document given by the man to his wife, or by the death of either party. Certain details, primarily as protections for the wife, were added in Talmudic times.[1]

Non-Orthodox developments have brought changes in who may marry whom. Intermarriage is often discouraged, though opinions vary.[2]

Overview

Historic view

In traditional Judaism, marriage is viewed as a contractual bond commanded by God in which a man and a woman come together to create a relationship in which God is directly involved. Though procreation is not the sole purpose, a Jewish marriage is traditionally expected to fulfil the commandment to have children.[3] In this view, marriage is understood to mean that the husband and wife are merging into a single soul, which is why a man is considered "incomplete" if he is not married, as his soul is only one part of a larger whole that remains to be unified.[4] HYPERLINK "https://en.wikipedia.org/wiki/Jewish_views_on_marriage#cite_note-5"[5]

Rashi explains the verse 'becoming one flesh' (of a man and a woman) as referring to children, whereas Nachmanides understands the verse as referring to sexual union/bonding. Both views are Orthodox and normative; both are interpretations of the Biblical verse discussing the union between a man and a woman.[*citation needed*]

Recent non-Orthodox views

Non-Orthodox Jewish denominations, such as Reconstructionist, Reform, and Conservative Judaism, recognize same-sex marriage, and de-emphasize procreation, focusing on marriage as a bond between a couple.[6] HYPERLINK "https://en.wikipedia.org/wiki/ Jewish_views_on_marriage#cite_note-7"[7] This view is considered as a diversion from the Jewish Law by the Orthodox denominations, rather than as a legitimate, alternative interpretation.

Betrothal and marriage

In Jewish law, marriage consists of two separate acts, called *erusin* or *kiddushin*,[a] which is the betrothal ceremony, and *nissu'in* or *chupah*, the actual Jewish wedding ceremony. *Erusin* changes the couple's personal circumstances, while *nissu'in* brings about the legal consequences of the change of circumstances. In Talmudic times, these two ceremonies usually took place up to a year apart; the bride lived with her parents until the actual marriage ceremony (*nissuin*), which would take place in a room or tent that the groom had set up for her. Since the Middle Ages the two ceremonies have taken place as a combined ceremony performed in public.[*citation needed*]

According to the Talmud,[8] *erusin* involves the groom handing an object to the bride – either an object of value such as a ring, or a document stating that she is being betrothed to him. In order to be valid, this must be done in the presence of two unrelated male witnesses. After *erusin*, the laws of adultery apply, and the marriage cannot be dissolved without a religious divorce. After *nisuin*, the couple may live together.

The act of *erusin* may be made by the intending parties or by their respective parents or other relatives on their behalf with their consent. A man and a woman cannot be betrothed to one another without agency and consent.[9] The act is formalized in a document known as the *Shtar Tena'im*, the "Document of Conditions" which is read prior to the *badekin*. After the reading, the mothers of the future bride and groom break a plate. Today, some sign the contract on the day of the wedding, some do it as an earlier ceremony, and some do not do it at all. It should also be emphasized that this practice is not explicitly mentioned in the Hebrew Bible.[*citation needed*]

In Haredi communities, marriages may be arranged by the parents of the prospective bride and groom, who may arrange a *shidduch* by engaging a professional match-maker (*shadchan*) who finds and introduces the prospective bride and groom and receives a fee for their services. The young couple is not forced to marry if either does not accept the other.[*citation needed*]

Matrimony

Marital harmony

Main article: Shalom bayit

Marital harmony, known as *shalom bayis*, is valued in Jewish tradition. The Talmud states that a man should love his wife as much as he loves himself, and honour her more than he honours himself;[10] indeed, one who honours his wife was said, by the classical rabbis, to be rewarded with wealth.[11] Similarly, a husband was expected to discuss with his wife any worldly matters that might arise in his life.[11] The Talmud forbids a husband from being overbearing to his household,[12] and domestic abuse by him was also condemned.[13] It was said of a wife that "God counts her tears".[13]

As for the wife, the greatest praise the Talmudic rabbis offered to any woman was that given to a wife who fulfils the wishes of her husband;[14] to this end, an early midrash states that a wife should not leave the home "too frequently".[15] A wife, also, was expected to be modest, even when alone with her husband.[16] God's presence dwells in a pure and loving home.[17]

Conjugal rights and obligations

Marriage obligations and rights in Judaism are ultimately based on those apparent in the Bible, which have been clarified, defined, and expanded on by many prominent rabbinic authorities throughout history.

Traditionally, the obligations of the husband include providing for his wife. He is obligated to provide for her sustenance for her benefit; in exchange, he is also entitled to her income. However, this is a right to the wife, and she can release her husband of the obligation of sustaining her, and she can then keep her income exclusively for herself. The document that provides for this is the *ketuba*.

The Bible itself gives the wife protections, as per Exodus 21:10,[18] although the rabbis may have added others later. The rights of the husband and wife are described in tractate *Ketubot* in the Talmud, which explains how the rabbis balanced the two sets of rights of the wife and the husband.

According to the non-traditional view, in the Bible the wife is treated as a possession owned by her husband,[19] but later Judaism imposed several obligations on the husband, effectively giving the wife several rights and freedoms;[19] indeed, being a Jewish wife was often a more favourable situation than being a wife in many other cultures.[19] For example, the Talmud establishes the principle that a wife is entitled, but not compelled, to the same dignity and social standing as her husband,[20] HYPERLINK "https://en.wikipedia.org/wiki/Jewish_ views_ on_marriage#cite_note-Ket61a-22"[21] and is entitled to keep any additional advantages she had as a result of her social status before her marriage.[20] HYPERLINK "https://en.wikipedia.org/ wiki/Jewish_views_on_marriage#cite_note-Ket61a-22"[21]

In the Bible

Biblical Hebrew has two words for "husband": *ba'al* (also meaning "master"), and *ish* (also meaning "man", parallel to *isha* meaning "woman" or "wife"). The words are contrasted in Hosea 2:16, where God speaks to Israel as though it is his wife: "On that day, says the Lord, you will call [me] 'my husband' (*ish*), and will no longer call me 'my master' (*ba'al*)."[22]

Early nomadic communities practised a form of marriage known as *beena*, in which a wife would own a tent of her own, within which she retains complete independence from her husband;[23] this principle appears to survive in parts of early Israelite society, as some early passages of the Bible appear to portray certain wives as each owning a tent as a personal possession[23] (specifically, Jael,[24] Sarah,[25] and Jacob's wives).[26] In later times, the Bible describes wives as being given the innermost room(s) of the husband's house, as her own private area to which men were not permitted;[27] in the case of wealthy husbands, the Bible describes their wives as having each been given an entire house for this purpose.[28]

It was not, however, a life of complete freedom. The descriptions of the Bible suggest that a wife was expected to perform certain household tasks: spinning, sewing, weaving, manufacture of clothing, fetching of water, baking of bread, and animal husbandry.[29] The Book of Proverbs contains an entire acrostic about the duties which would be performed by a virtuous wife. [30]

The husband, too, is indirectly implied to have responsibilities to his wife. The Torah obligates a man to not deprive his wife of food, clothing, or of sexual activity (*onah*);[31] if the husband does not provide the first wife with these things, she is to be divorced, without cost to her.[32] The Talmud interprets this as a requirement for a man to provide food and clothing to, and have sex with, each of his wives, even if he only has one.[13]

As a polygynous society, the Israelites did not have any laws which imposed monogamy on men.[33] HYPERLINK "https:// en.wikipedia. org/wiki/Jewish_views_on_marriage#cite_note-JewEncAdu-35"[34] Adulterous married and betrothed women, as well as their male accomplices, were subject to the death penalty by the biblical laws against adultery.[35] According to the Book of Numbers, if a woman was suspected of adultery, she was to be subjected to the ordeal of the bitter water,[36] a form of trial by ordeal, but one that took a miracle to convict. The literary prophets indicate that adultery was a frequent occurrence, despite their strong protests against it,[37] and these legal strictnesses.[33]

In the Talmud and Rabbinic Judaism

The Talmud sets a minimum provision which a husband must provide to his wife:[13]

- Enough bread for at least two meals a day

- Sufficient oil for cooking and for lighting purposes

- Sufficient wood for cooking

- Fruit and vegetables

- Wine, if it is customary in the locality for women to drink it

- Three meals on each shabbat consisting of fish and meat

- An allowance of a silver coin (Hebrew: *ma'ah*) each week Rabbinic courts could compel the husband to make this provision, if he fails to do so voluntarily.[38] The Chatam Sofer, a prominent 19th century halachic decisor, argued that if a man could not provide his wife with this minimum, he should be compelled to divorce her;[39] other Jewish rabbis argued that a man should be compelled to hire himself out, as a day-labourer, if he cannot otherwise make this provision to his wife.[13]

According to prominent Jewish writers of the Middle Ages, if a man is absent from his wife for a long period, the wife should be allowed to sell her husband's property, if necessary to sustain herself.[40] HYPERLINK "https://en.wikipedia.org/wiki/Jewish_views_on_marriage#cite_note-JabAshEbEz70-42"[41] Similarly, they argued that if a wife had to take out a loan to pay for her sustenance during such absence, her husband had to pay the debt on his return.[40] HYPERLINK "https://en.wikipedia.org/wiki/Jewish_views_on_marriage#cite_note-JabAshEbEz70-42"[41]

In order to offset the husband's duty to support his wife, she was required by the Talmud to surrender all her earnings to her husband, together with any profit she makes by accident, and the right of usufruct on her property;[42] the wife was not required to do this if she wished to support herself.[42] Although the wife always retained ownership of her property itself, if she died while still married to her husband, he was to be her heir, according to the opinion of the Talmud;[42] this principle, though, was modified, in various ways, by the rabbis of the Middle Ages.[13]

Home and household

In Jewish tradition, the husband was expected to provide a home for his wife, furnished in accordance to local custom and appropriate to his status;[13] the marital couple were expected to live together in this home, although if the husband's choice of work made it difficult to do so, the Talmud excuses him from the obligation.[43] Traditionally, if the husband changed his usual abode, the wife was considered to have a duty to move with him.[13] In the Middle Ages, it was argued that if a person continued to refuse to live with their spouse, the spouse in question had sufficient grounds for divorce.[44] HYPERLINK "https://en.wikipedia.org/wiki/Jewish_views_on_marriage#cite_note-46"[45]

Most Jewish religious authorities held that a husband must allow his wife to eat at the same table as him, even if he gave his wife enough money to provide for herself.[13] By contrast, if a husband mistreated his wife, or lived in a disreputable neighbourhood, the Jewish religious authorities would permit the wife to move to another home elsewhere, and would compel the husband to finance her life there.[13]

Expanding on the household tasks which the Bible implies a wife should undertake,[19] rabbinic literature requires her to perform all the housework (such as baking, cooking, washing, caring for her children, etc.), unless her marriage had given the husband a large dowry;[13] in the latter situation, the wife was expected only to tend to "affectionate" tasks, such as making his bed and serving him his food.[13] Jewish tradition expected the husband to provide the bed linen and kitchen utensils.[13] If the wife had young twin children, the Talmud made her husband responsible for caring for one of them.[46]

Clothing

The Talmud elaborates on the biblical requirement of the husband to provide his wife with clothing, by insisting that each year he must provide each wife with 50 zuzim's-worth of clothing,[47] including garments appropriate to each <u>season</u> of the year.[13] The Talmudic rabbis insist that this annual clothing gift should include one hat, one belt, and three pairs of shoes[48] (one pair for each of the three main annual festivals: <u>Passover</u>, <u>Shabu</u> HYPERLINK "https://en.wikipedia. org/wiki/Shabu%27ot"' HYPERLINK "https://en.wikipedia.org/wiki/ Shabu%27ot"<u>ot</u>, and <u>Sukkoth</u>).[47] The husband was also expected by the classical rabbis to provide his wife with jewelry and perfumes if he lived in an area where this was customary.[13]

Physical obligations

The Talmud argues that a husband is responsible for the protection of his wife's body. If his wife became ill, then he would be compelled, by the Talmud, to defray any medical expense which might be incurred in relation to this;[42] the Talmud requires him to ensure that the wife receives care. [42] Although he technically had the right to divorce his wife, enabling him to avoid paying for her medical costs, several prominent rabbis throughout history condemned such a course of action as inhuman behaviour, even if the wife was suffering from a prolonged illness.[13]

If the wife dies, even if not due to illness, the Talmud's stipulations require the husband to arrange, and pay for, her burial;[49] the burial must, in the opinion of the Talmud, be one conducted in a manner befitting the husband's social status, and in accordance with the local custom.[49] Prominent rabbis of the Middle Ages clarified this, stating that the husband must make any provisions required by local burial customs, potentially including the hiring of mourners and the erection of a tombstone. [50] HYPERLINK "https://en.wikipedia.org/ wiki/Jewish_ views_on_marriage#cite_note-JabAshEbEz89-52"[51] According to the Talmud, and later rabbinic writers, if the husband was absent, or refused to do these things, a rabbinical court should arrange the wife's funeral, selling some of the husband's property in order to defray the costs.[50] HYPERLINK "https:// en.wikipedia.org/ wiki/Jewish_views_on_marriage#cite_note-JabAshEbEz89-52"[51]

If the wife was captured, the husband was required by the Talmud and later writers to pay the ransom demanded for her release;[52] HYPERLINK "https://en.wikipedia.org/wiki/Jewish_ views_on_ marriage#cite_note-MaMiTorIs141822-54"[53] HYPERLINK "https://en.wikipedia.org/wiki/Jewish_views_ on_marriage#cite_note-JabAshEbEz78-55"[54] HYPERLINK "https://en.wikipedia.org/wiki/Jewish_views_on_ marriage#cite_note-JKShuArYD25210-56"[55] there is some debate whether the husband was required only to pay up to the wife's market value as a slave,[56] or whether he must pay any ransom, even to the point of having to sell his possessions to raise the funds.[13] If the husband and wife were both taken captive, the historic Jewish view was that the rabbinic courts should first pay the ransom for the wife, selling some of the husband's property in order to raise the funds. [52] HYPERLINK "https:// en.wikipedia.org/wiki/Jewish_views_on_ marriage#cite_ note-MaMiTorIs141822-54"[53] HYPERLINK "https:// en.wikipedia.org/wiki/Jewish_views_on_marriage#cite_ note- JabAshEbEz78-55"[54] HYPERLINK "https:// en.wikipedia.org/wiki/Jewish_views_on_marriage#cite_note-JKShuArYD25210-56"[55]

Fidelity

In the classical era of the rabbinic scholars, the death penalty for adultery was rarely applied. It forbids conviction if:

- the woman had been raped, rather than consenting to the crime;[57]

- the woman had mistaken the paramour for her husband;[34]

- the woman was unaware of the laws against adultery before she committed the crime;[34]

- the woman had not been properly warned. This requires that the two witnesses testifying against her warn her that the Torah prohibits adultery; that the penalty for adultery is death; and that she immediately responded that she is doing so with full knowledge of those facts. Even if she was warned, but did not acknowledge those facts immediately upon hearing them, and immediately before doing the act, she is not put to death. These conditions apply in all death- penalty convictions.[58]

These rules made it practically impossible to convict any woman of adultery; in nearly every case, women were acquitted.[34] However, due to the belief that a priest should be untainted, a Kohen was compelled to divorce his wife if she had been raped.[34] HYPERLINK "https:// en.wikipedia.org/wiki/Jewish_ views_on_marriage#cite_note-60"[59]

In Talmudic times, once the death penalty was no longer enforced for any crime,[60] even when a woman was convicted, the punishment was comparatively mild: adulteresses were flogged instead.[34] Nevertheless, the husbands of convicted adulteresses were not permitted by the Talmud to forgive their guilty wives, instead being compelled to divorce them;[61] according to Maimonides, a conviction for adultery nullified any right that the wife's marriage contract (Hebrew: *ketubah*) gave her to a compensation payment for being divorced.[62]

Once divorced, an adulteress was not permitted, according to the Talmudic writers, to marry her paramour.[63]

As for men who committed adultery (with another man's wife), Abba ben Joseph and Abba Arika are both quoted in the Talmud as expressing abhorrence, and arguing that such men would be condemned to Gehenna.[64]

Family purity

Main article: Niddah

The laws of "family purity" (*taharat hamishpacha*) are considered an important part of an Orthodox Jewish marriage, and adherence to them is (in Orthodox Judaism) regarded as a prerequisite of marriage. This involves observance of the various details of the menstrual *niddah* laws. Orthodox brides and grooms attend classes on this subject prior to the wedding. The niddah laws are regarded as an intrinsic part of marital life (rather than just associated with women). Together with a few other rules, including those about the ejaculation of semen, these are collectively termed "family purity".

Sexual relations

In marriage, conjugal relations are guaranteed as a fundamental right for a woman, along with food and clothing.[65] This obligation is known as *onah*.[66] Sex within marriage is the woman's right, and the man's duty. The husband is forbidden from raping his wife, they are not to be intimate while drunk or while either party is angry at the other. A woman should be granted a *get* (divorce) if she seeks it because her husband is disgusting or loathsome to her. If either partner consistently refuses to participate, that person is considered rebellious, and the other spouse can sue for divorce.[67]

Age of marriage

Citing the primacy of the divine command given in Genesis 1:28, the time between puberty and age twenty has been considered the ideal time for men and women to be wed in traditional Jewish thought. Some rabbis have gone further to commend the age of eighteen as most ideal, while others have advocated for the time immediately following puberty, closer to the age of fourteen, essentially "as early in life as possible."[68] Babylonian rabbis understood marriage as God's means of keeping male sexuality from going out of control, so they advocated for early marriage to prevent men from succumbing to temptation in their youth.[69] Some commended early marriage for its benefits: Rabbi Hisda maintained that early marriage could lead to increased intelligence.[68]

A large age gap between spouses, in either direction, is advised against as unwise.[70] A younger woman marrying a significantly older man however is especially problematic: marrying one's young daughter to an old man was declared as reprehensible as forcing her into prostitution.[71] Moreover, it is problematic for an older man to be unmarried in the first place. Marriage is held to be uniquely mandatory for men, and an unmarried man over the age of twenty is considered "cursed by God Himself."[68]

There is evidence however that in some communities males did not marry until "thirty or older."[72] In medieval Jewish Ashkenazi communities, women continued to be married young.[73] Since the Enlightenment, young marriage has become rarer among Jewish communities.[74]

Consent

According to the Talmud, a father is commanded not to marry his daughter to anyone until she grows up and says, "I want this one". [75] A marriage that takes place without the consent of the girl is not an effective legal marriage. [76]

A *ketannah* (literally meaning "little [one]") was any girl between the age of 3 years and that of 12 years plus one day; [77] she was subject to her father's authority, and he could arrange a marriage for her without her agreement. [77] However, after reaching the age of maturity, she would have to agree to the marriage to be considered as married. [78] HYPERLINK "https://en.wikipedia. org/wiki/Jewish_views_on_ marriage#cite_note-80" [79] If the father was dead or missing, the brothers of the *ketannah*, collectively, had the right to arrange a marriage for her, as had her mother. [77] In these situations, a *ketannah* would always have the right to annul her marriage, even if it was the first. [80]

If the marriage did end (due to divorce or the husband's death), any further marriages were optional; the *ketannah* retained her right to annul them. [80] The choice of a *ketannah* to annul a marriage, known in Hebrew as *mi'un* (literally meaning "refusal", "denial", "protest"), [80] led to a true annulment, not a divorce; a divorce document (*get*) was not necessary, [81] and a *ketannah* who did this was not regarded by legal regulations as a divorcee, in relation to the marriage. [82] Unlike divorce, *mi'un* was regarded with distaste by many rabbinic writers, [80] even in the Talmud; [83] in earlier classical Judaism, one major faction — the House of Shammai — argued that such annulment rights only existed during the betrothal (not engagement) period (*erusin*) and not once the actual marriage (*nissu* HYPERLINK "https://en.wikipedia. org/wiki/Nissuin"' HYPERLINK " https:// en.wikipedia.org/wiki/ Nissuin"in) had begun. [84]

Intermarriage

Main article: <u>Interfaith marriage in Judaism</u>

Rates of marriage between Jews and non-Jews have increased in countries other than Israel (the <u>Jewish diaspora</u>). According to the <u>National Jewish Population Survey 2000-01</u>, 47% of marriages involving Jews in the United States between 1996 and 2001 were with non-Jewish partners. Jewish leaders in different branches generally agree that possible assimilation is a crisis, but they differ on the proper response to <u>intermarriage</u>.

Attitudes

Further information: <u>Conservative Halakha § Restrictions on marriage</u>

- All branches of <u>Orthodox Judaism</u> do not sanction the validity or legitimacy of intermarriages.

- <u>Conservative Judaism</u> does not sanction intermarriage, but encourages acceptance of the non-Jewish spouse within the family, hoping that such acceptance will lead to conversion.

- <u>Reform Judaism</u> and <u>Reconstructionist Judaism</u> permit total personal autonomy in interpretation of <u>Jewish Law</u>, and intermarriage is not forbidden. Reform and Reconstructionist rabbis are free to take their own approach to performing marriages between a Jewish and non-Jewish partner. Many, but not all, seek agreement from the couple that the children will be raised as Jewish.

There are also differences between streams on what constitutes an intermarriage, arising from their <u>differing criteria for being</u>

Jewish in the first place. Orthodox Jews do not accept as Jewish a person whose mother is not Jewish, nor a convert whose conversion was conducted under the authority of a more liberal stream.

Marriage in Israel

See also: Marriage in Israel

In Israel, the only institutionalized form of Jewish marriage is the religious one, i.e., a marriage conducted under the auspices of the rabbinate. Specifically, marriage of Israeli Jews must be conducted according to Jewish Law (*halakha*), as viewed by Orthodox Judaism. One consequence is that Jews in Israel who cannot marry according to Jewish law (e.g., a *kohen* and a divorcée, or a Jew and one who is not halachically Jewish), cannot marry each other. This has led for calls, mostly from the secular segment of the Israeli public, for the institution of civil marriage.[*citation needed*]

Some secular-Jewish Israelis travel abroad to have civil marriages, either because they do not wish an Orthodox wedding or because their union cannot be sanctioned by *halakha*. These marriages are legally recognized by the State, but are not recognized by the State Rabbinate.

Marriages performed in Israel must be carried out by religious authorities of an official religion (Judaism, Islam, Christianity, or Druze), unless both parties are without religion.

Divorce

Halakha (Jewish Law) allows for divorce. The document of divorce is termed a *get*. The final divorce ceremony involves the husband giving the *get* document into the hand of the wife or her agent, but the wife may sue in rabbinical court to initiate the divorce. In such a case, a husband may be compelled to give the *get*, if he has violated any of his numerous obligations; [*which?*] this was traditionally accomplished by beating and or monetary coercion. [*citation needed*] The rationale was that since he was required to divorce his wife due to his (or her) violations of the contract, his good inclination desires to divorce her, and the community helps him to do what he wants to do anyway. In this case, the wife may or may not be entitled to a payment.

Since around the 12th century, Judaism recognized the right of a wife abused physically or psychologically to a divorce. [*citation needed*]

Conservative Judaism follows halacha, although differently than Orthodox Judaism. Reform Jews usually use an egalitarian form of the *Ketubah* at their weddings. They generally do not issue Jewish divorces, seeing a civil divorce as both necessary and sufficient; however, some Reform rabbis encourage the couple to go through a Jewish divorce procedure. Orthodox Judaism does not recognize civil law as overriding religious law, and thus does not view a civil divorce as sufficient. Therefore, a man or woman may be considered divorced by the Reform Jewish community, but still married by the Conservative community. Orthodox Judaism usually does not recognize Reform weddings because according to Talmudic law, the witnesses to the marriage must be Jews who observe *halakha*, which is seldom the case in reform weddings. [*citation needed*]

Agunah

Main article: Agunah

Traditionally, when a husband fled, or his whereabouts were unknown for any reason, the woman was considered an *agunah* (literally "an anchored woman"), and was not allowed to remarry; in traditional Judaism, divorce can only be initiated by the husband. Prior to modern communication, the death of the husband while in a distant land was a common cause of this situation. In modern times, when a husband refuses to issue a *get* due to money, property, or custody battles, the woman who cannot remarry is considered a *Mesorevet get*, not an agunah. A man in this situation would not be termed a *Misarev Get* (literally, "a refuser of a divorce document"), unless a legitimate Beis Din had required him to issue a Get. The term *agunah* is often used in such circumstances, but it is not technically accurate.

Within both the Conservative and Orthodox communities, there are efforts to avoid situations where a woman is not able to obtain a Jewish divorce from her husband. The *ketubah* serves this function in Conservative Judaism in order to prevent husbands from refusing to give their wives a divorce. To do this, the *ketubah* has built in provisions; so, if predetermined circumstances occur, the divorce goes into effect immediately. [85] After the fact, various Jewish and secular legal methods are used to deal with such problems. None of the legal solutions addresses the *agunah* problem in the case of a missing husband.

Same-sex marriage

See also: Homosexuality and Judaism

In antiquity

The Midrash is one of the few ancient religious texts that makes reference to same-sex marriage. The following teaching can be found twice in the Midrash:

> Rabbi Huna said in the name of Rabbi Joseph, 'The generation of the Flood was not wiped out until they wrote תויסמומג (either sexual hymns or marriage documents) for the union of a man to a male or to an animal.'
>
> — Genesis Rabbah 26:5; Leviticus Rabbah 23:9 HYPERLINK "https://en.wikipedia.org/wiki/ Jewish_ views_ on_ marriage#cite_ note-87"[86]

Another important reference is found in the Babylonian Talmud:

> 'Ula said: Non-Jews [literally Bnei Noach, the progeny of Noah] accepted upon themselves thirty mitzvot [divinely ordered laws], but they only abide by three of them: The first one is that they do not write marriage documents for male couples, the second one is that they do not sell dead [human] meat by the pound in stores, and the third one is that they respect the Torah.'
>
> — Chullin 92ab[87]

In Orthodox Judaism

Orthodox Judaism does not have a Jewish legal construct of same- gender marriage. While any two Jewish adults may be joined by a Jewish legal contract, the rites of *kiddushin* are reserved for a union of a man and woman. Orthodox Judaism does not recognize civil marriages to have theological legal standing, be they civil marriages between male and female, or between two adults of the same gender.

In Conservative Judaism

In June 2012, the American branch of <u>Conservative Judaism</u> formally approved same-sex marriage ceremonies in a 13–0 vote with one abstention.[88]

In Reform Judaism

In 1996, the <u>Central Conference of American Rabbis</u> passed a resolution approving same-sex civil marriage. However, this same resolution made a distinction between civil marriages and religious marriages; this resolution thus stated:

> However we may understand homosexuality, whether as an illness, as a genetically based dysfunction or as a sexual preference and lifestyle – we cannot accommodate the relationship of two homosexuals as a "marriage" within the context of Judaism, for none of the elements of *qiddushin* (sanctification) normally associated with marriage can be invoked for this relationship.[89]

> The Central Conference of American Rabbis support the right of gay and lesbian couples to share fully and equally in the rights of civil marriage, and That the

CCAR oppose governmental efforts to ban gay and lesbian marriage.

That this is a matter of civil law, and is separate from the question of rabbinic officiation at such marriages. [*attribution needed*]

In 1998, an ad hoc CCAR committee on human sexuality issued its majority report (11 to 1, 1 abstention) which stated that the holiness within a Jewish marriage "may be present in committed same gender relationships between two Jews and that these relationships can serve as the foundation of stable Jewish families, thus adding strength to the Jewish community." The report called for CCAR to support rabbis in officiating at same-sex marriages. Also in 1998, the Responsa Committee of the CCAR issued a lengthy *teshuvah* (rabbinical opinion)[90] that offered detailed argumentation in support of both sides of the question whether a rabbi may officiate at a commitment ceremony for a same-sex couple.

In March 2000, CCAR issued a new resolution stating that "We do hereby resolve that the relationship of a Jewish, same gender couple is worthy of affirmation through appropriate Jewish ritual, and further resolve, that we recognize the diversity of opinions within our ranks on this issue. We support the decision of those who choose to officiate at rituals of union for same-sex couples, and we support the decision of those who do not."

In Reconstructionist Judaism

The Reconstructionist Rabbinical Association (RRA) encourages its members to officiate at same-sex marriages, though it does not require it of them.

Buddhist view of marriage

From Wikipedia, the free encyclopedia

Korean <u>bride</u> HYPERLINK "https://en.wikipedia.org/wiki/Hwarot"' HYPERLINK "https://en.wikipedia.org/wiki/Hwarot"<u>s robe</u>

The **Buddhist view of marriage** considers marriage a secular affair[1] and as such, it is not considered a <u>sacrament</u>.[2] Buddhists are expected to follow the civil laws regarding marriage laid out by their respective governments.[2]

While the ceremony itself is civil, many Buddhists obtain the blessing from monks at the local temple after the marriage is completed.[1]

History

<u>Gautama Buddha</u> never spoke against marriage[3] but instead pointed out some of the difficulties of marriage.[3] He is quoted in the Parabhava <u>Sutta</u> as saying

> Not to be contented with one's own wife, and to be seen with harlots and the wives of others -- this is a cause of one's downfall. Being past one's youth, to take a young wife and to be unable to sleep for jealousy of her -- this is a cause of one's downfall.[4]

Views

The Pali Canon, a major Theravada text, bars both male and female monastics from both heterosexual and homosexual activities. While homosexuality may or may not be explicitly condemned in some texts, according to the <u>Dalai Lama</u>:

"From a Buddhist point of view, physical touching between men-to-men and women-to-women is generally considered sexual misconduct."[5]

While <u>Buddhism</u> may neither encourage nor discourage getting married, itdoes provideprinciplesregardingit.[6] HYPERLINK"https:// en.wikipedia.org/wiki/Buddhist_view_ of_marriage#cite_note-7"[7]

The Digha Nikaya 31 (<u>Sigalovada Sutta</u>) describes the respect that one is expected to give to one's spouse.[8]

In Tibetan Buddhism

The <u>Dalai Lama</u> has spoken of the merits of marriage:

Too many people in the West have given up on marriage. They don't understand that it is about developing a mutual admiration of someone, deep respect and trust, and awareness of another human's needs...The new easy-come, easy-go relationships give us more freedom -- but less contentment.[9]

Divorce

Since marriage is secular,[1] Buddhism has no restrictions on divorce. [10]<u>Ven. K. Sri Dhammananda</u> has said "if a husband and wife really cannot live together, instead of leading a miserable life and harboring more jealousy, anger and hatred, they should have the liberty to separate and live peacefully."[11]

Christian views on marriage

From Wikipedia, the free encyclopedia

Bride and groom outside a church in Amalfi, Italy

From the earliest days of the <u>Christian faith</u>, Christians have honored *holy matrimony* (as Christian <u>marriages</u> are referred to) as a divinely blessed, lifelong, <u>monogamous</u> union between a man and a woman. According to the Episcopal <u>Book of Common Prayer</u> (1979), reflecting the traditional view, "Christian marriage is a solemn and public covenant between a man and a woman in the presence of God,"[1] "intended by God for their mutual joy; for the help and comfort given one another in prosperity and adversity; and, when it is God's will, for the procreation of children and their nurture."[2] However, while many Christians might agree with the traditional definition, the terminology and theological views of marriage have varied through time in different countries, and among Christian denominations.

Many <u>Protestants</u> consider marriage to be a sacred institution or "holy ordinance" of God. <u>Roman Catholics</u> and <u>Eastern Orthodox Christians</u> consider marriage as a <u>holy sacrament</u> or <u>sacred mystery</u>. However, there have been differing attitudes among denominations and individual Christians towards not only the concept of <u>Christian marriage</u>, but also concerning <u>divorce</u>, <u>remarriage</u>, <u>gender roles</u>, family authority (the "<u>headship</u>" of the husband), the <u>legal status of married women</u>, <u>birth control</u>, <u>marriageable age</u>, <u>cousin marriage</u>, <u>marriage of in-laws</u>, <u>interfaith marriage</u>, <u>same-sex marriage</u>, and <u>polygamy</u>, among other topics, so that in the 21st century there cannot be said to be a single, uniform, worldwide view of marriage among all who profess to be Christians.

Christian teaching has never held that marriage is necessary for everyone; for many centuries in <u>Western Europe</u>, priestly or monastic <u>celibacy</u> was valued as highly as, if not higher than, marriage. Christians who did not marry were expected to refrain from all <u>sexual activity</u>, as were those who took <u>holy orders</u> or <u>monastic vows</u>.

In <u>some Western countries</u>, a separate and <u>secular</u> civil wedding ceremony is required for recognition by the state, while in other Western countries, couples must merely obtain a <u>marriage license</u> from a local government authority and can be married by Christian or other <u>clergy</u> if they are authorized by law to conduct weddings. In this case, the state recognizes the religious marriage as a <u>civil marriage</u> as well; and Christian couples married in this way have all the rights of civil marriage, including, for example, <u>divorce</u>, even if their <u>church forbids divorce</u>.

Since the beginning of the 21st century, same-sex couples have been allowed to <u>marry civilly</u> in many countries, and some Christian churches in those countries allow <u>religious marriage of same-sex couples</u>, though others forbid it, along with <u>all other same-sex relationships</u>.

Biblical foundations and history

Christians believe that marriage is considered in its ideal according to the purpose of <u>God</u>. At the heart of God's design for marriage is companionship and intimacy.

The biblical picture of marriage expands into something much broader, with the husband and wife relationship illustrating the relationship between <u>Christ and the church</u>.

It is also considered in its actual occurrence, sometimes involving failure. Therefore, the Bible speaks on the subject of divorce.[3] The New Testament recognizes a place for singleness. <u>Salvation</u> within Christianity is not dependent on the continuation of a biological lineage.[4]

Old Testament

See also: <u>Polygamy § Judaism</u>, and <u>Pilegesh</u>

The Genesis creation account tells the story of when God instituted marriage. This took place after the creation of the first woman, Eve, from Adam, the first man.[5]

> The Lord God said, "It is not good for the man to be alone. I will make a helper suitable for him."

> Now the Lord God had formed out of the ground all the wild animals and all the birds in the sky. He brought them to the man to see what he would name them; and whatever the man called each living creature, that was its name. So the man gave names to all the livestock, the birds in the sky and all the wild animals.

> But for Adam no suitable helper was found. So the Lord God caused the man to fall into a deep sleep; and while he was sleeping, he took one of the man's ribs and then closed up the place with flesh. Then the Lord God made a woman from the rib he had taken out of the man, and he brought her to the man.

> The man said,

"This is now bone of my bones and flesh of my flesh; she shall be called 'woman,' for she was taken out of man."

That is why a man leaves his father and mother and is united to his wife, and they become one flesh.

— Genesis 2:18-24, NIV[6]

Polygyny, or men having multiple wives at once, is one of the most common marital arrangements represented in the Old Testament,[7] yet scholars doubt that it was common among average Israelites because of the wealth needed to practice it.[8] Both the biblical patriarchs and kings of Israel are described as engaged in polygamous relationships.[9] Despite the various polygynous relationships in the Bible, Old Testament scholar Peter Gentry has said that it does not mean that God condones polygyny. He also made note of the various problems that polygynous relationships present with the examples of Abraham, Jacob, David, and Solomon in the Bible.[10] Alternatively, this could be a case of graded absolutism.

Betrothal (*erusin*), which is merely a binding promise to get married, is distinct from marriage itself (*nissu* HYPERLINK "https://en.wikipedia. org/wiki/Nissuin"' HYPERLINK " https:// en.wikipedia.org/wiki/ Nissuin"in), with the time between these events varying substantially. [7] HYPERLINK "https:// en.wikipedia.org/wiki/Christian_views_on_ marriage#cite_ note-CheyneAndBlackMar-11"[11] Nonetheless, when a couple is betrothed, they are held accountable to the laws against adultery, like an officially married couple. From this, it is implied that a couple is considered to be married even they've only betrothed.[12] Since a wife was regarded as property in biblical times, the betrothal (*erusin*) was effected simply by purchasing her from her father (or guardian) (i.e. paying the bride price to the woman and her father);[7] HYPERLINK "https://en.wikipedia.org/wiki/Christian_views_ on_marriage#cite_note-CheyneAndBlackMar-11"[11] the woman's consent is not explicitly required by any biblical law. Nonetheless, in one Biblical story, Rebecca was asked whether she agreed to be married before the marriage took place.[11] HYPERLINK "https://en.wikipedia.org/wiki/Christian_views_on_marriage#cite_note- 13"[13] Additionally, according to French anthropologist Philippe Rospabé, the payment of the bride price does not entail the purchase of a woman, as was thought in the early twentieth century. Instead, it is a purely symbolic gesture acknowledging (but never paying off) the husband's permanent debt to the wife's parents.[14]

Rembrandt's depiction of Samson's marriage feast

Like the adjacent Arabic culture (in the pre-Islamic period),[15] the act of marriage appears mainly to have consisted of the groom fetching the bride, although among the Israelites the procession was a festive occasion, accompanied by music, dancing, and lights. [7] HYPERLINK "https://en.wikipedia.org/wiki/Christian_ views_ on_marriage#cite_note-CheyneAndBlackMar-11"[11] To celebrate the marriage, week-long feasts were sometimes held. [7] HYPERLINK "https://en.wikipedia.org/wiki/Christian_ views_on_marriage#cite_ note-CheyneAndBlackMar-11"[11]

In Old Testament times, a wife was submissive to her husband, which may interpreted as Israelite society viewing wives as the chattel of husbands. [7] HYPERLINK "https://en.wikipedia.org/wiki/Christian_views_on_ marriage#cite_note-CheyneAndBlackMar-11"[11] The descriptions of the Bible suggest that she would be expected to perform tasks such as spinning, sewing, weaving, manufacture of clothing, fetching of water, baking of bread, and animal husbandry.[16] However, wives were usually looked after with care, and <u>bigamous</u> men were expected to ensure that they give their first wife food, clothing, and sexual activity.[17]

Since a wife was regarded as property, her husband was originally free to divorce her with little restriction, at any time. [11] A divorced couple could get back together unless the wife had married someone else after her divorce.[18]

Jesus on marriage, divorce, and remarriage

Sometimes used as a <u>symbol</u> for Christian marriage: Two gold wedding rings interlinked with the Greek letters *chi* (X) and *rho* (P)— the first two letters in the Greek word for "Christ" (see <u>Labarum</u>)

The Bible clearly addresses marriage and divorce. Those in troubled marriages are encouraged to seek counseling and restoration because, according to some advocates of traditional marriage ethics, most divorces are neither necessary nor unavoidable.[19]

> "Have you not read that at the beginning the Creator made them male and female, and said, "For this reason a man will leave his father and mother and be united to his wife, and the two will become one flesh"? So they *are* no longer two, but one. Therefore, what God has joined together, let no one separate."
>
> —   HYPERLINK "https://en.wikipedia.org/wiki/ Christian views on marriage#cite note-20"[20]

In the gospels of both Matthew and Mark, Jesus appealed to God's will in creation. He builds upon the narratives in where male and female are created together[21] and for one another.[22] Thus Jesus takes a firm stance on the permanence of marriage in the original will of God. This corresponds closely with the position of the Pharisee school of thought led by Shammai, at the start of the first millennium,[23] HYPERLINK "https://en.wikipedia.org/wiki/Christian_views_on_marriage#cite_note-24"[24] HYPERLINK "https://en.wikipedia.org/wiki/Christian_views_on_ marriage#cite_note-25"[25] with which Jesus would have been familiar. By contrast, Rabbinic Judaism subsequently took the opposite view, espoused by Hillel, the leader of the other major Pharisee school of thought at the time; in Hillel's view, men were allowed to divorce their wives for any reason.[23]

Some hold that marriage vows are unbreakable, so that even in the distressing circumstances in which a couple separates, they are still married from God's point of view. This is the Roman Catholic church's position, although occasionally the church will declare a marriage to be "null" (in other words, it never really was a marriage). [26] William Barclay (1907-1978) has written:

> There is no time in history when the marriage bond stood in greater peril of destruction than in the days when Christianity first came into this world. At that time the world was in danger of witnessing the almost total break-up of marriage and the collapse of the home Theoretically no nation ever had a higher ideal of marriage than the Jews had. The voice of God had said, "I hate divorce"[27]

> — William Barclay[28]

Jesus brought together two passages from Genesis, reinforcing the basic position on marriage found in Jewish scripture. Thus, he implicitly emphasized that it is God-made ("God has joined together"), "male and female,"[28] lifelong ("let no one separate"), and monogamous ("a man his wife").[29]

Jesus used the image of marriage and the family to teach the basics about the Kingdom of God. He inaugurated his ministry by blessing the wedding at Cana. In the Sermon on the Mount he set forth a new commandment concerning marriage, teaching that lustful looking constitutes adultery.[30] He also superseded a Mosaic Law allowing divorce with his teaching that "… anyone who divorces his wife, except for sexual immorality (Gk. *porneia*),[31] causes her to become an adulteress, and anyone who marries the divorced woman commits adultery".[32] Similar Pauline teachings are found in Corinthians 7.[33] The exception clause—"except for…"—uses the Greek word *porneia* which is variously translated "fornication" (KJV), "marital unfaithfulness" (NIV 1984), "sexual immorality" (NIV 2011), "unchastity" (RSV), *et al. The KJV New Testament Greek Lexicon, KJV says porneia* includes a variety of sexual "deviations" to include "illicit sexual intercourse, adultery, fornication, homosexuality, lesbianism, intercourse with animals, etc., sexual intercourse with close relatives "[34]

Theologian Frank Stagg says that manuscripts disagree as to the presence in the original text of the phrase "except for fornication". [29]:pp.300–301 Stagg writes: "Divorce always represents failure a deviation from God's will There is grace and redemption where there is contrition and repentance. There is no clear authorization in the New Testament for remarriage after divorce." Stagg interprets the chief concern of Matthew 5 as being "to condemn the criminal act of the man who divorces an innocent wife. Jesus was rebuking the husband who victimizes an innocent wife and thinks that he makes it right with her by giving her a divorce". He points out that Jesus refused to be trapped by the <u>Pharisees</u> into choosing between the strict and liberal positions on divorce as held at the time in Judaism. When they asked him, "Is it lawful for a man to divorce his wife for any cause?"[35] he answered by reaffirming God's will as stated in Genesis,[36] that in marriage husband and wife are made "one flesh", and what God has united man must not separate. [37] HYPERLINK "https://en.wikipedia.org/wiki/Christian_ views_on_marriage#cite_ note-Stagg_NT-29"[29]:pp.300–301

There is no evidence that Jesus himself ever married, and considerable evidence that he remained single. In contrast to Judaism and many other traditions,[4]:p.283 he taught that there is a place for voluntary singleness in Christian service. He believed marriage could be a distraction from an urgent mission,[38] that he was living in a time of crisis and urgency where the <u>Kingdom of God</u> would be established where there would be no marriage nor giving in marriage:

> "I tell you the truth," Jesus said to them, "no one who has left home or wife or brothers or parents or children for the sake of the kingdom of God will fail to receive many times as much in this age and, in the <u>age to come</u>, <u>eternal life</u>."

> — HYPERLINK "<u>https://en.wikipedia.org/wiki/ Christian views on marriage#cite note-39</u>"[39]

In Matthew 22, Jesus is asked about the continuing state of marriage after death and he affirms that at the resurrection "people neither marry nor be given in marriage; they are like the angels in heaven.".

New Testament beyond the Gospels

Saint Paul Writing His Epistles, 16th century.

The Apostle Paul quoted passages from Genesis almost verbatim in two of his New Testament books. He used marriage not only to describe the kingdom of God, as Jesus had done, but to define also the nature of the 1st-century Christian church. His theological view was a Christian development of the Old Testament parallel between marriage and the relationship between God and Israel. He analogized the church as a bride and Christ as the bridegroom—drawing parallels between Christian marriage and the relationship between Christ and the Church.

There is no hint in the New Testament that Jesus was ever married, and no clear evidence that Paul was ever married. However, both Jesus and Paul seem to view marriage as a legitimate calling from God for Christians. Paul elevates singleness to that of the preferable position, but does offer a caveat suggesting this is "because of the impending crisis"—which could itself extend to present times (see also Pauline privilege).[40] Paul's primary issue was that marriage adds concerns to one's life that detract from their ability to serve God without distraction.[41] HYPERLINK "https://en.wikipedia.org/wiki/ Christian_views_on_marriage#cite_note-42"[42]

Some scholars have speculated that Paul may have been a widower since prior to his conversion to Christianity he was a Pharisee and member of the Sanhedrin, positions in which the social norm of the day required the men to be married. But it is just as likely that he never married at all.[43]

Yet, Paul acknowledges the mutuality of marital relations, and recognizes that his own singleness is "a particular gift from

God" that others may not necessarily have. He writes: "Now to the unmarried and the widows I say: It is good for them to stay unmarried, as I am. But if they cannot control themselves, they should marry, for it is better to marry than to burn with passion."[44]

Paul indicates that bishops, deacons, and elders must be "husbands of one wife", and that women must have one husband. This is usually understood to legislate against polygamy rather than to require marriage:

> Now the overseer (bishop) is to be above reproach, faithful to his wife, temperate, self-controlled, respectable, hospitable, able to teach, not given to drunkenness, not violent but gentle, not quarrelsome, not a lover of money.[45]

> A deacon must be faithful to his wife and must manage his children and his household well.[46]

> The reason I left you in Crete was that you might put in order what was left unfinished and appoint (or ordain) elders in every town, as I directed you. An elder must be blameless, faithful to his wife, a man whose children believe and are not open to the charge of being wild and disobedient.[47]

In the Roman Age, female widows who did not remarry were considered more pure than those who did.[48] Such widows were known as *one man woman* (*enos andros gune*) in the epistles of Paul. [49] Paul writes:

> No widow may be put on the list of widows unless she is over sixty, has been faithful to her husband, and is

well known for her good deeds, such as bringing up children, showing hospitality, washing the feet of the Lord's people, helping those in trouble and devoting herself to all kinds of good deeds".[50]

Paul allowed widows to remarry.[51] Paul says that only one-man women older than 60 years[50] can make the list of Christian widows who did special tasks in the community, but that younger widows should remarry to hinder sin.

Marriage and early Church Fathers

Building on what they saw the example of Jesus and Paul advocating, some early Church Fathers placed less value on the family and saw celibacy and freedom from family ties as a preferable state.

Nicene Fathers such as Augustine believed that marriage was a sacrament because it was a symbol used by Paul to express Christ's love of the Church. However, there was also an apocalyptic dimension in his teaching, and he was clear that if everybody stopped marrying and having children that would be an admirable thing; it would mean that the Kingdom of God would return all the sooner and the world would come to an end.[52] Such a view reflects the Manichaean past of Augustine.

While upholding the New Testament teaching that marriage is "honourable in all and the bed undefiled,"[53] Augustine believed that "yet, whenever it comes to the actual process of generation, the very embrace which is lawful and honourable cannot be effected without the ardour of lust...This is the carnal concupiscence, which, while it is no longer accounted sin in the regenerate, yet in no case happens to nature except from sin."[54]

Both Tertullian and Gregory of Nyssa were church fathers who were married. They each stressed that the happiness of marriage was ultimately rooted in misery. They saw marriage as a state of bondage that could only be cured by celibacy. They wrote that at the very least, the virgin woman could expect release from the "governance of a husband and the chains of children."[55]:p.151

Tertullian argued that second marriage, having been freed from the first by death,"will have to be termed no other than a species of fornication," partly based on the reasoning that this involves desiring to marry a woman out of sexual ardor, which a Christian convert is to avoid.[56]

Also advocating celibacy and virginity as preferable alternatives to marriage, Jerome wrote: "It is not disparaging wedlock to prefer virginity. No one can make a comparison between two things if one is good and the other evil."[57] On First Corinthians 7:1 he reasons, "It is good, he says, for a man not to touch a woman. If it is good not to touch a woman, it is bad to touch one: for there is no opposite to goodness but badness. But if it be bad and the evil is pardoned, the reason for the concession is to prevent worse evil."[58]

St. John Chrysostom wrote: "...virginity is better than marriage, however good.... Celibacy is...an imitation of the angels. Therefore, virginity is as much more honorable than marriage, as the angel is higher than man. But why do I say angel? Christ, Himself, is the glory of virginity."[59]

Cyprian, Bishop of Carthage, said that the first commandment given to men was to increase and multiply, but now that the earth was full there was no need to continue this process of multiplication.[60]

This view of marriage was reflected in the lack of any formal liturgy formulated for marriage in the early Church. No special ceremonial was devised to celebrate Christian marriage—despite the fact that the Church had produced liturgies to celebrate the Eucharist, Baptism and Confirmation. It was not important for a couple to have their nuptials blessed by a priest. People could marry by mutual agreement in the presence of witnesses.[52]

At first, the old Roman pagan rite was used by Christians, although modified superficially. The first detailed account of a Christian wedding in the West dates from the 9th century. This system, known as Spousals, persisted after the Reformation.[52]

Denominational beliefs and practice

Further information: Wedding § Christian customs, and Marriage § Christianity

Marriage and Christianity

Main article: Fornication § Christianity

Catholicism

Main article: Catholic marriage

Crowning during Holy Matrimony in the Syro-Malabar Catholic Church which is an Eastern Catholic Church and a part of the Saint Thomas Christian community in India.

Catholic couple at their Holy Matrimony or marriage. In the Latin Rite of the Catholic Church, during the celebration the priest imposes his liturgical stole upon the couple's hands, as a sign to confirm the marriage bond.

Today all <u>Christian</u> denominations regard marriage as a sacred institution, a covenant. Roman Catholics consider it to be a <u>sacrament</u>. [61] Marriage was officially recognized as a sacrament at the 1184 Council of Verona.[62] HYPERLINK "https://en.wikipedia.org/wiki/Christian_views_on_marriage#cite_note-monger-63"[63] Before then, no specific ritual was prescribed for celebrating a marriage: "Marriage vows did not have to be exchanged in a church, nor was a priest's presence required. A couple could exchange consent anywhere, anytime."[63] HYPERLINK "https://en.wikipedia.org/wiki/ Christian_views_on_marriage#cite_note-64"[64]

In the decrees on marriage of the <u>Council of Trent</u> (twenty-fourth session from 1563), the validity of marriage was made dependent upon the wedding taking place before a priest and two witnesses,[63] HYPERLINK "https://en.wikipedia.org/wiki/Christian_views_on_ marriage#cite_note-omalley-65"[65] although the lack of a requirement for parental consent ended a debate that had proceeded from the 12th century.[65] In the case of a divorce, the right of the innocent party to marry again was denied so long as the other party was alive, even if the other party had committed adultery.[65]

The Catholic Church allowed marriages to take place inside churches only starting with the 16th century, beforehand religious marriages happened on the porch of the church.[63]

The <u>Roman Catholic Church</u> teaches that God himself is the author of the sacred institution of marriage, which is His way of showing love for those He created. Marriage is a divine institution that can never be broken, even if the husband or wife legally divorce in the civil courts; as long as they are both alive, the Church considers them bound together by God. Holy Matrimony is another name for sacramental marriage. Marriage is intended to be a faithful, exclusive, lifelong union of a man and a woman. Committing themselves completely to each other, a Catholic husband and wife strive to sanctify each other, bring children into the world, and educate them in the Catholic way of life. Man and woman, although created differently from each other, complement each other. This complementarity draws them together in a mutually loving union.[66]

The valid marriage of baptized Christians is one of the seven Roman Catholic sacraments. The sacrament of marriage is the only sacrament that a priest does not administer directly; a priest, however, is the chief witness of the husband and wife's administration of the sacrament to each other at the wedding ceremony in a Catholic church.

The Roman Catholic Church views that Christ himself established the sacrament of marriage at the wedding feast of Cana; therefore, since it is a divine institution, neither the Church nor state can alter the basic meaning and structure of marriage. Husband and wife give themselves totally to each other in a union that lasts until death.[67]

Arbëreshë Albanian couple during marriage in an Italo-Greek Catholic Church rite.

Priests are instructed that marriage is part of God's natural law and to support the couple if they do choose to marry. Today it is common for Roman Catholics to enter into a "mixed marriage" between a Catholic and a baptized non-Catholic. Couples entering into a mixed marriage are usually allowed to marry in a Catholic church provided their decision is of their own accord and they intend to remain together for life, to be faithful to each other, and to have children which are brought up in the Catholic faith.[68]

During the Warsaw Uprising (1944), a Polish couple, members of an Armia Krajowa resistance group, are married in a secret Catholic chapel in a street in Warsaw.

In Roman Catholic teaching, marriage has two objectives: the good of the spouses themselves,[69] and the procreation and education of children (1983 code of canon law, c.1055; 1994 catechism, par.2363). Hence "entering marriage with the intention of never having children is a grave wrong and more than likely grounds for an annulment."[70] It is normal procedure for a priest to ask the prospective bride and groom about their plans to have children before officiating at their wedding. The Roman Catholic Church may refuse to marry anyone unwilling to have children, since procreation by "the marriage act" is a fundamental part of marriage.[71] Thus usage of any form of contraception, in vitro fertilization, or birth control besides natural family planning is a grave offense against the sanctity of marriage and ultimately against God.[71]

Protestantism

Wedding ceremony at First Baptist Church of Rivas, Baptist Convention of Nicaragua, 2011

The Wedding of Stephen Beckingham and Mary Cox by William Hogarth, c. 1729 (Metropolitan Museum of Art, N.Y.).

Purposes

Most Protestant denominations hold marriage to be ordained by God for the union between a man and a woman. They see the primary purposes of this union as intimate companionship, rearing children and mutual support for both husband and wife to fulfill their life callings.[72] Protestant Christian denominations consider marital sexual pleasure to be a gift of God, though they vary on their position on birth control, ranging from the acceptance of the use of contraception to only allowing natural family planning to teaching Quiverfull doctrine—that birth control is sinful and Christians should have large families. [73] HYPERLINK "https:// en.wikipedia.org/wiki/Christian_ views_on_marriage#cite_note-Joyce2009-74"[74] Conservative Protestants consider marriage a solemn covenant between wife, husband and God. Most view sexual relations as appropriate only within a marriage. Protestant Churches discourage divorce though the way it is addressed varies by denomination; for example, the Reformed Church in America permits divorce and remarriage,[75] while connexions such as the Evangelical Methodist Church Conference forbid divorce except in the case of fornication and do not allow for remarriage in any circumstance.[76] HYPERLINK "https://en.wikipedia.org/wiki/ Christian_views_on_marriage#cite_note-77"[77]

Many Methodist Christians teach that marriage is "God's gift and covenant intended to imitate God HYPERLINK "https:// en.wikipedia. org/wiki/New_Covenant'" HYPERLINK "https://en.wikipedia. org/wiki/New_Covenant"s covenant with humankind"[78] that "Christians enter in their baptism."[79] For example, the rite used in the Free Methodist Church proclaims that marriage is "more than a legal contract, being a bond of union made in heaven, into which you enter discreetly and reverently."[78]

Roles and responsibilities

Roles and responsibilities of husband and wives now vary considerably on a continuum between the long-held male dominant/female submission view and a shift toward equality (without sameness)[80] of the woman and the man.[81] There is considerable debate among many Christians today—not just Protestants—whether equality of husband and wife or male headship is the biblically ordained view, and even if it is biblically permissible. The divergent opinions fall into two main groups: Complementarians (who call for husband-headship and wife-submission) and Christian Egalitarians (who believe in full partnership equality in which couples can discover and negotiate roles and responsibilities in marriage).[82]

There is no debate that Ephesians 5 presents a historically benevolent husband-headship/wife-submission model for marriage. The questions are (a) how these New Testament household codes are to be reconciled with the calls earlier in Chapter 5 (cf. verses 1, 18, 21) for mutual submission among all believers, and (b) the meaning of "head" in v.23. It is important to note that verse 22 contains no verb in the original manuscripts,[83] which were also not divided into verses:[3] Ephesians 5 (NIV)

1 Follow God's example, therefore, as dearly loved children 2 and walk in the way of love....

18 be filled with the Spirit....

Submit to one another out of reverence for Christ.

22 Wives, *[submit yourselves]* to your own husbands as you do to the Lord. 23 For the husband is the head of the wife as Christ is the head of the church, his body, of which he is the Savior. 24 Now as the church submits to Christ, so also wives should submit to their husbands in everything.

25 Husbands, love your wives, just as Christ loved the church and gave himself up for her 26 to make her holy, cleansing her

by the washing with water through the word, 27 and to present her to himself as a radiant church, without stain or wrinkle or any other blemish, but holy and blameless. 28 In this same way, husbands ought to love their wives as their own bodies. He who loves his wife loves himself. 29 After all, no one ever hated their own body, but they feed and care for their body, just as Christ does the church— 30 for we are members of his body. 31 "For this reason a man will leave his father and mother and be united to his wife, and the two will become one flesh." 32 This is a profound mystery—but I am talking about Christ and the church. 33 However, each one of you also must love his wife as he loves himself, and the wife must respect her husband.

Eastern Orthodoxy

Main article: Marriage in the Eastern Orthodox Church

The Wedding of Nicholas II and Grand Duchess Alexandra Feodorovna, by Ilya Yefimovich Repin, 1894 (Russian State Museum, St. Petersburg).

In the Eastern Orthodox Church, marriage is treated as a Sacred Mystery (sacrament), and as an ordination. It serves to unite a woman and a man in eternal union before God. [84] HYPERLINK "https:// en.wikipedia.org/wiki/Christian_ views_on_marriage#cite_note- 85"[85] HYPERLINK "https:// en.wikipedia.org/wiki/Christian_ views_on_marriage#cite_ note-ReferenceA-86"[86] It refers to the 1st centuries of the church, where spiritual union of spouses in the first sacramental marriage was eternal.[86] HYPERLINK "https:// en.wikipedia. org/wiki/Christian_views_on_marriage#cite_note- 87"[87] Therefore, it is considered a martyrdom as each spouse learns to die to self for the sake of the other. Like all Mysteries, Orthodox marriage is more than just a celebration of something which already exists: it is the creation of something new, the imparting to the couple of the grace which transforms them from a 'couple' into husband and wife within the Body of Christ.[88]

Byzantine wedding ring, depicting Christ uniting the bride and groom, 7th century, nielloed gold (Musée du Louvre).

Marriage is an icon (image) of the relationship between Jesus and the Church. This is somewhat akin to the Old Testament prophets' use of marriage as an analogy to describe the relationship between God and Israel. Marriage is the simplest, most basic unity of the church: a congregation where "two or three are gathered together in Jesus' name."[89] HYPERLINK "https://en.wikipedia.org/wiki/   Christian_views_on_marriage#cite_note-Grabbe-88"[88] The home is considered a consecrated space (the ritual for the Blessing of a House is based upon that of the Consecration of a Church), and the husband and wife are considered the ministers of that congregation. However, they do not "perform" the Sacraments in the house church; they "live" the Sacrament of Marriage. Because marriage is considered to be a pilgrimage wherein the couple walk side by side toward the Kingdom of Heaven, marriage to a non-Orthodox partner is discouraged, though it may be permitted.

Unlike Western Christianity, Eastern Christians do not consider the sacramental aspect of the marriage to be conferred by the couple themselves. Rather, the marriage is conferred by the action of the Holy Spirit acting through the priest. Furthermore, no one besides a bishop or priest—not even a deacon—may perform the Sacred Mystery.

The external sign of the marriage is the placing of wedding crowns upon the heads of the couple, and their sharing in a "Common Cup" of wine. Once crowned, the couple walk a circle three times in a ceremonial "dance" in the middle of the church, while the choir intones a joyous three-part antiphonal hymn, "Dance, Isaiah"

The sharing of the Common Cup symbolizes the transformation of their union from a common marriage into a sacred union. The wedding is usually performed after the Divine Liturgy at which the couple receives Holy Communion. Traditionally, the wedding couple would wear their wedding crowns for eight days, and there is a special prayer said by the priest at the removal of the crowns.

Divorce is discouraged. Sometimes out of *economia* (mercy) a marriage may be dissolved if there is no hope whatever for a marriage to fulfill even a semblance of its intended sacramental character.[88] The standard formula for remarriage is that the Orthodox Church joyfully blesses the first marriage, merely performs the second, barely tolerates the third, and invariably forbids the fourth.[90] "On the basis of the ideal of the first marriage as an image of the glory of God the question is which significance such a second marriage has and whether it can be regarded as Mysterion. Even though there are opinions (particularly in the west) which deny the sacramental character to the second marriage, in the orthodox literature almost consistently either a reduced or even a full sacramentality is attributed to it. The investigation of the second marriage rite shows that both positions affirming the sacramentality to a second marriage can be justified."[91]

Orthodox Church prepared for a wedding (Hagia Sophia, Thessaloniki.)

Early church texts forbid marriage between an Orthodox Christian and a heretic or schismatic (which would include all non-Orthodox Christians). Traditional Orthodox Christians forbid mixed marriages with other denominations. More liberal ones perform them, provided that the couple formally commit themselves to rearing their children in the Orthodox faith.

All people are called to celibacy—human beings are all born into virginity, and Orthodox Christians are expected by Sacred Tradition to remain in that state unless they are called into marriage and that call is sanctified.[88] The church blesses two paths on the journey to salvation: monasticism and marriage. Mere celibacy, without the sanctification of monasticism, can fall into selfishness and tends to be regarded with disfavour by the Church.[88]

Orthodox priests who serve in parishes are usually married. They must marry prior to their ordination. If they marry after they are ordained they are not permitted to continue performing sacraments. If their wife dies, they are forbidden to remarry; if they do, they may no longer serve as a priest. A married man may be ordained as a priest or deacon. However, a priest or deacon is not permitted to enter into matrimony after ordination. Bishops must always be monks and are thus celibate. However, if a married priest is widowed, he may receive monastic tonsure and thus become eligible for the episcopate.

The Eastern Orthodox Church believes that marriage is an eternal union of spouses, but in Heaven there will not be a procreative bond of marriage.

Oriental Orthodoxy

The Non-Chalcedonian Churches of Oriental Orthodoxy hold views almost identical to those of the (Chalcedonian) Eastern

Orthodox Church. The Coptic Orthodox Church allows second marriages only in cases of adultery or death of spouse.[92]

Non-Trinitarian denominations

A Celestial Marriage must be performed in an LDS temple.

The Church of Jesus Christ of Latter-day Saints

See also: Marriage in The Church of Jesus Christ of Latter-day Saints and Mormonism and polygamy

In the teachings of the Church of Jesus Christ of Latter-day Saints (LDS Church), celestial (or eternal) marriage is a covenant between a man, a woman, and God performed by a priesthood authority in a temple of the church.[93] Celestial marriage is intended to continue forever into the afterlife if the man and woman do not break their covenants. [93] Thus, eternally married couples are often referred to as being "sealed" to each other. Sealed couples who keep their covenants are also promised to have their posterity sealed to them in the afterlife. [93] (Thus, "families are forever" is a common phrase in the LDS Church.) A celestial marriage is considered a requirement for exaltation.[93]

In some countries, celestial marriages can be recognized as civil marriages; in other cases, couples are civilly married outside of the temple and are later sealed in a celestial marriage.[94] (The church will no longer perform a celestial marriage for a couple unless they are first or simultaneously legally married.) The church encourages its members to be in good standing with it so that they may marry or be sealed in the temple. A celestial marriage is not annulled by a civil divorce: a "cancellation of a sealing" may be granted, but only by the First Presidency, the highest authority in the church. Civil divorce and marriage outside the temple carries somewhat of a stigma in the Mormon culture; the church teaches that the "gospel of Jesus Christ—including repentance, forgiveness, integrity, and love—provides the remedy for conflict in marriage."[95] Regarding marriage and divorce, the church instructs its leaders: "No priesthood officer is to counsel a person whom to marry. Nor should he counsel a person to divorce his or her spouse. Those decisions must originate and remain with the individual. When a marriage ends in divorce, or if a husband and wife separate, they should always receive counseling from Church leaders."[96]

In church temples, members of the LDS Church perform vicarious celestial marriages for deceased couples who were legally married.

New Church (or Swedenborgian Church)

The New Church teaches that marital love (or "conjugial love") is "the precious jewel of human life and the repository of the Christian religion" because the love shared between a husband and a wife is the source of all peace and joy.[97] Emanuel Swedenborg coined the term "conjugial" (rather than the more usual adjective in reference to marital union, "conjugal"[98] HYPERLINK "https://en.wikipedia. org/wiki/ Christian_views_on_marriage#cite_note-Dictionary. reference. com-99"[99]) to describe the special love experienced by married partners.[100] HYPERLINK "https://en.wikipedia.org/wiki/ Christian_views_on_marriage#cite_note-Dictionary.reference. com-99"[99] When a husband and wife work together to build their marriage on earth, that marriage continues after the deaths of their bodies and they live as angels in heaven into eternity. Swedenborg claimed to have spoken with angelic couples who had been married for thousands of years.[101] Those who never married in the natural world will, if they wish, find a spouse in heaven.

Interdenominational marriage

In Christianity, an <u>interdenominational marriage</u> (also known as an ecumenical marriage) is a marriage between two baptized Christians who belong to different <u>Christian denominations</u>, e.g. a wedding between a Lutheran Christian man and a Catholic Christian woman. Nearly all Christian denominations permit interdenominational marriages.[104]

In <u>Methodism</u>, ¶81 of the 2014 *Discipline* of the <u>Allegheny Wesleyan Methodist Connection</u>, states with regard to interdenominational marriages: "We do not prohibit our people from marrying persons who are not of our connection, provided such persons have the form and are seeking the power of godliness; but we are determined to discourage their marrying persons who do not come up to this description."[105]

The Catholic Church recognizes as sacramental, (1) the marriages between two baptized Protestants or between two baptized Orthodox Christians, as well as (2) marriages between baptized non-Catholic Christians and Catholic Christians,[106] although in the latter case, consent from the diocesan bishop must be obtained, with this being termed "permission to enter into a mixed marriage".[107] To illustrate (1), for example, "if two Lutherans marry in the Lutheran Church in the presence of a Lutheran minister, the Catholic Church recognizes this as a valid sacrament of marriage."[106] Weddings in which both parties are Catholic Christians are ordinarily held in a Catholic church, while weddings in which one party is a Catholic Christian and the other party is a non-Catholic Christian can be held in a Catholic church or a non-Catholic Christian church.[108]

Interreligious marriage

Main article: Interfaith marriage in Christianity

In Christianity, an interfaith marriage is a marriage between a baptized Christian and a non-baptized person, e.g. a wedding between a Christian man and Jewish woman.[104]

In the Presbyterian Church (USA), the local church congregation is tasked with supporting and including an interfaith couple with one being a baptized Presbyterian Christian and the other being a non- Christian, in the life of the Church, "help[ing] parents make and live by commitments about the spiritual nurture of their children", and being inclusive of the children of the interfaith couple.[109] The pastor is to be available to help and counsel the interfaith couple in their life journey.[109]

Although the Catholic Church recognizes as natural marriages weddings between two non-Christians or those between a Catholic Christian and a non-Christian, these are not considered to be sacramental, and in the latter case, the Catholic Christian must seek permission from his/her bishop for the marriage to occur; this permission is known as "dispensation from disparity of cult".[110]

In Methodist Christianity, the 2014 *Discipline* of the Allegheny Wesleyan Methodist Connection discourages interfaith marriages, stating "Many Christians have married unconverted persons. This has produced bad effects; they have either been hindered for life, or have turned back to perdition."[105] Though the United Methodist Church authorizes its clergy to preside at interfaith marriages, it notes that Corinthians 6 has been interpreted "as at least an ideal if not an absolute ban on such [interfaith] marriages as an issue of scriptural faithfulness, if not as an issue of Christian survival."[111] At the same time, for those already in an interfaith marriage (including cases in which there is a non-Christian couple and one party converts to Christianity after marriage), the Church notes that Saint Paul "addresses persons married to unbelievers and encourages them to stay married."[112] HYPERLINK "https://en.wikipedia.org/wiki/Christian_ views_on_marriage#cite_ note-BurtonEdwards2010-111"[111]

Same-sex marriage

Main articles: Blessing of same-sex unions in Christian churches and *Same-sex marriage*

Anglican denominations such as the Episcopal Church in United States HYPERLINK "https://en.wikipedia.org/wiki/Christian_views_ on_marriage#cite_note-113"[113] the Anglican Church of Canada,[114] the Anglican Church in Aotearoa, New Zealand and Polynesia,[115] the Anglican Episcopal Church of Brazil,[116] the Scottish Episcopal Church in Scotland[117] and mainline Protestant denominations such as the United Church of Christ,[118] the United Church of Canada, the Metropolitan Community Church,[119] the Presbyterian Church (USA),[120] the Quakers,[121] the United Reformed Church in United Kingdom,[122] the Church of Scotland,[123] the Methodist Church of Great Britain,[124] the Church of Iceland,[125] the Church of Sweden,[126] the Church of Denmark,[127] the Church of Norway,[128] the United Protestant Church in Belgium,[129] the Protestant Church in Baden,[130] the Evangelical Church in Berlin, Brandenburg and Silesian Upper Lusatia,[131] the Evangelical Church of Bremen, the Evangelical Lutheran Church in Brunswick,[132] the Evangelical Church of Hesse Electorate-Waldeck,[133] the Evangelical Lutheran Church in Oldenburg,[134] the Evangelical Lutheran Church of Hanover,[135] the Church of Lippe,[136] the Evangelical Reformed Church in Bavaria and Northwestern Germany,[137] HYPERLINK "https://en.wikipedia. org/wiki/Christian_views_on_marriage#cite_note-138"[138] the Evangelical Church in the Rhineland,[139] the Protestant Church in Hesse and Nassau,[140] the Evangelical Lutheran Church in Northern Germany HYPERLINK "https://en.wikipedia.org/wiki/Christian_ views_on_marriage#cite_note-141"[141] the Protestant Church of the Palatinate,[142] the Evangelical Church of Westphalia,[143] the Mennonite Church in the Netherlands HYPERLINK "https://en.wikipedia. org/wiki/Christian_views_on_marriage#cite_note-144"[144] the United Protestant Church of France,[145] the Catholic Diocese of the Old Catholics in Germany,[146] the Christian Catholic Church of Switzerland,[147] some Reformed churches in Federation of Swiss Protestant Churches for example the Reformed Church of Aargau,[148] the Protestant Church of Geneva HYPERLINK "https://en.wikipedia.org/wiki/Christian_views_on_ marriage#cite_note-149"[149] or the Evangelical Reformed Church of the Canton of Zürich HYPERLINK "https://en.wikipedia.org/wiki/Christian_views_on_marriage#cite_ note-150"[150] and some non-trinitarian denominations such as the Unity Church and the Unitarians,[120] some international evangelical denominations, such as the Association of Welcoming and Affirming Baptists HYPERLINK "https://en.wikipedia.org/wiki/Christian_ views_on_marriage#cite_note-151"[151] and Affirming Pentecostal Church International HYPERLINK "https://en.wikipedia.org/wiki/ Christian_views_on_marriage#cite_note-152"[152] perform weddings between same-sex couples.

The Evangelical Lutheran Church of America, the Evangelical Lutheran Church in Canada, some Lutheran and united churches in Evangelical Church in Germany, some Reformed churches in Federation of Swiss Protestant Churches, and the

Protestant Church in the Netherlands HYPERLINK "https://en.wikipedia.org/wiki/   Christian_views_on_marriage#cite_note-153"[153] do not administer sacramental marriage to same-sex couples, but blesses same-sex unions through the use of a specific liturgy.[154]

The Roman Catholic Church, the Orthodox Christian Church, and other more conservative Protestant denominations do not perform or recognize same-sex marriage because they do not consider it as marriage at all, and considering any homosexual sexual activity to be sinful. The Global Anglican Future Conference (GAFCON) consisting of the Church of Nigeria, Anglican Church of Kenya, Anglican Church of Tanzania, Rwanda and Uganda; Anglican Church of South America, Australia, parts of England, Canada, USA and Church of India through the Jerusalem Conference clearly asserted "the unchangeable standard of Christian marriage between one man and one woman as the proper place for sexual intimacy."[155]

Location of the wedding

With respect to religion, historic Christian belief emphasizes that Christian weddings should occur in a church as Christian marriage should begin where one also starts their faith journey (Christians receive the sacrament of baptism in church in the presence of their congregation).[156] Catholic Christian weddings must "take place in a church building" as holy matrimony is a sacrament; sacraments normatively occur in the presence of Christ in the house of God, and "members of the faith community [should be] present to witness the event and provide support and encouragement for those celebrating the sacrament."[156] Bishops never grant permission "to those requesting to be married in a garden, on the beach, or some other place outside of the church" and a dispensation is only granted "in extraordinary circumstances (for example, if a bride or groom is ill or disabled and unable to come to the church)."[156] Marriage in the church, for Christians, is seen as contributing to the fruit of the newlywed couple regularly attending church each Lord HYPERLINK "https://en.wikipedia.org/ wiki/ Lord%27s_Day'" HYPERLINK "https://en.wikipedia.org/ wiki/ Lord%27s_Day"s Day and raising children in the faith.[156]

Theological views

Christians seek to uphold the seriousness of wedding vows. Yet, they respond with compassion to deep hurts by recognizing that divorce, though less than the ideal, is sometimes necessary to relieve one partner of intolerable hardship, unfaithfulness or desertion.[3] While the voice of God had said, "I hate divorce",[157] some authorities believe the divorce rate in the church is nearly comparable to that of the culture at large.[19]

Christians today hold three competing views as to what is the biblically ordained relationship between husband and wife. These views range from Christian egalitarianism that interprets the New Testament as teaching complete equality of authority and responsibility between the man and woman in marriage, all the way to Patriarchy that calls for a "return to complete patriarchy" in which relationships are based on male-dominant power and authority in marriage:[158]

1. Christian Egalitarians believe in an equal partnership of the wife and husband with neither being designated as the leader in the marriage or family. Instead, the wife and husband share a fully equal partnership in both their marriage and in the family. Its proponents teach "the fundamental biblical principle of the equality of all human beings before God".

"There is neither Jew nor Gentile, neither slave nor free, nor is there male and female, for you are all one in Christ Jesus."[159]

According to this principle, there can be no moral or theological justification for permanently granting or denying status, privilege, or prerogative solely on the basis of a person's race, class, or gender.[160]

2. Christian Complementarians prescribe husband-headship—a male-led hierarchy. This view's core beliefs call for a husband's "loving, humble headship" and the wife's "intelligent, willing submission" to his headship. They believe women have "different but complementary roles and responsibilities in marriage".[161]

3. Biblical patriarchy, though not at all popular among mainstream Christians, prescribes a strict male-dominant hierarchy. A very strong view makes the husband the ruler over his wife and his household.[162] Their organization's first tenet is that "God reveals Himself as masculine, not feminine. God is the eternal Father and the eternal Son, the Holy Spirit is also addressed as He, and Jesus Christ is a male". They consider the husband-father to be sovereign over his household—the family leader, provider, and protector. They call for a wife to be obedient to her head (her husband).[158]

Some Christian authorities permit the practice polygamy (specifically polygyny), but this practice, besides being illegal in Western cultures, is now considered to be out of the Christian mainstream in most parts of the globe; the Lutheran World Federation hosted a regional conference in Africa, in which the acceptance of polygamists and their wives into full membership by the Lutheran Church in Liberia was defended as being permissible. [163] While the Lutheran Church in Liberia permits men to retain their wives if they married them prior to being received into the Church, it does not permit polygamists who have become Christians to marry more wives after they have received the sacrament of Holy Baptism.[164]

Family authority and responsibilities

Orthodox betrothal depicted by Vasily Vladimirovich Pukirev, 1862.

Much of the dispute hinges on how one interprets the New Testament household code *(Haustafel)*, a term coined by Martin Luther, which has as its main focus hierarchical relationships between three pairs of social classes that were controlled by Roman law: husbands/wives, parents/children, and masters/slaves. The apostolic teachings, with variations, that constitute what has been termed the "household code" occurs in four epistles (letters) by the Apostle Paul and in 1 Peter.

In the early Roman Republic, long before the time of Christ, the law of *manus* along with the concept of *patria potestas* (rule of the fathers), gave the husband nearly absolute autocratic power over his wife, children, and slaves, including the power of life and death. In practice, the extreme form of this right was seldom exercised, and it was eventually limited by law.[165]

Theologian Frank Stagg HYPERLINK "https://en.wikipedia. org/wiki/   Christian_views_on_marriage#cite_note-Stagg-166"[166]: pp.187ff finds the basic tenets of the code in Aristotle's discussion of the household in Book 1 of *Politics* and in Philo's *Hypothetica 7.14.*[167] Serious study of the New Testament Household Code *(Haustafel)* began with Martin Dilbelius in 1913, with a wide range of studies since then. In a Tübingen dissertation,[168] by James E. Crouch concludes that the early Christians found in Hellenistic Judaism a code which they adapted and Christianized.

The Staggs believe the several occurrences of the New Testament household code in the Bible were intended to meet the needs for *order* within the churches and in the society of the day. They maintain that the New Testament household code is an attempt by Paul and Peter to Christianize the concept of family relationships for Roman citizens who had become followers of Christ. The Staggs write that there is some suggestion in scripture that because Paul had taught that they had newly found freedom "in Christ", wives, children, and slaves were taking improper advantage of the *Haustafel* both in the home and the church. "The form of the code stressing reciprocal social duties is traced to Judaism's own Oriental background, with its strong moral/ethical demand but also with a low view of woman At bottom is probably to be seen the perennial tension between freedom and order What mattered to (Paul) was 'a new creation'[169] and 'in Christ' there is 'not any Jew not Greek, not any slave nor free, not any male and female'.[159] HYPERLINK "https://en.wikipedia.org/wiki/   Christian_views_on_marriage#cite_note-Staggs-3"[3]

Two of these Christianized codes are found in Ephesians 5 (which contains the phrases "husband is the head of the wife" and "wives, submit to your husband") and in Colossians 3, which instructs wives to subordinate themselves to their husbands.

The importance of the meaning of "head" as used by the Apostle Paul is pivotal in the conflict between the Complementarian position and the Egalitarian view. The word Paul used for "head", transliterated from Greek, is *kephalē*. Today's English word "cephalic" (/sə'fælɪk/ sə- FAL-ik) stems from the Greek *kephalē* and means "of or relating to the head; or located on, in, or near the head." A thorough concordance search by Catherine Kroeger shows that the most frequent use of "head" (*kephalē*) in the New Testament is to refer to "the anatomical head of a body". She found that its second most frequent use in the New Testament was to convey the metaphorical sense of "source". [170] HYPERLINK "https://en.wikipedia.org/wiki/Christian_ views_ on_marriage#cite_note-171"[171] Other Egalitarian authors such as Margaret Howe agree with Kroeger, writing that "The word 'head'[172] must be understood not as 'ruler' but as 'source'".[173]

Wayne Grudem criticizes commonly rendering *kephalē* in those same passages only to mean "source", and argues that it denotes "authoritative head" in such texts as Corinthians 11. They interpret that verse to mean that God the father is the authoritative head over the Son, and in turn Jesus is the authoritative head over the church, not simply its source. By extension, they then conclude that in marriage and in the church, the man is the authoritative head over the woman.[174]

Another potential way to define the word "head", and hence the relationship between husband and wife as found in the Bible, is through the example given in the surrounding context in which the word is found.[175] In that context the husband and wife are compared to Christ and his church. The context seems to imply an authority structure based on a man sacrificing himself for his wife, as Christ did for the church; a love-based authority structure, where submission is not required but freely given based on the care given to the wife.[176]

Some biblical references on this subject are debated depending on one's school of theology. The historical grammatical method is a hermeneutic technique that strives to uncover the meaning of the text by taking into account not just the grammatical words, but also the syntactical aspects, the cultural and historical background, and the literary genre. Thus references to a patriarchal Biblical culture may or may not be relevant to other societies. What is believed to be a timeless truth to one person or denomination may be considered a cultural norm or minor opinion to another.

Egalitarian view

See also: Christian egalitarianism

Christian Egalitarians (from the French word "égal" meaning "equal") believe that Christian marriage is intended to be a marriage without any hierarchy—a full and equal partnership between the wife and husband. They emphasize that nowhere in the New Testament is there a requirement for a wife to *obey* her husband. While "obey" was introduced into marriage vows for much of the church during the Middle Ages, its only New Testament support is found in Peter 3, with that only being by implication from Sarah's obedience to Abraham. [3]:p.190 Scriptures such as Galatians 3:28 state that in Christ, right relationships are restored and in him, "there is neither Jew nor Greek, slave nor free, male nor female."[177]

Christian Egalitarians interpret scripture to mean that God intended spouses to practice *mutual submission*, each in equality with the other. The phrase "mutual submission" comes from a verse in Ephesians 5 which precedes advice for the three domestic relationships of the day, including slavery. It reads, "Submit to one another ('mutual submission') out of reverence for Christ", wives to husbands, children to parents, and slaves to their master. Christian Egalitarians believe that full partnership in marriage is the most biblical view, producing the most intimate, wholesome, and reciprocally fulfilling marriages.[178]

The Christian Egalitarian view[179] of marriage asserts that gender, in and of itself, neither privileges nor curtails a believer's gifting or calling to any ministry in the church or home. It does not imply that women and men are identical or undifferentiated, but affirms that God designed men and women to complement and benefit one another.[180] A foundational belief of Christian Egalitarians is that the husband and wife are created equally and are ordained of God to "become one", a biblical principle first ordained by God in Genesis 2, reaffirmed by Jesus in Matthew 19 and Mark 10, and by the Apostle Paul in Ephesians 5. Therefore, they see that "oneness" as pointing to gender equality in marriage. They believe the biblical model for Christian marriages is therefore for the spouses to share equal responsibility within the family—not one over the other nor one under the other.

David Dykes, theologian, author, and pastor of a 15,000-member Baptist church, sermonized that "When you are in Christ, you have full equality with all other believers". In a sermon he entitled "The Ground Is Level at the Foot of the Cross", he said that some theologians have called one particular Bible verse the Christian *Magna Carta*. The Bible verse reads: "There is neither Jew nor Gentile, neither slave nor free, nor is there male and female, for you are all one in Christ Jesus."[181] Acknowledging the differences between men and women, Dykes writes that "in Christ, these differences don't define who we are. The only category that really matters in the world is whether you are **in Christ**. At the cross, Jesus destroyed all the made- made[*clarification needed*] barriers of hostility:" ethnicity, social status, and gender.[182]

The Galatians 3 passage comes after the apostle Paul tells us he would not submit to what was "hypocritical" to the Gospel.[183] The apostle Peter had affirmed the truth of the Gospel regarding the Gentiles with his words, but his actions compromised it.[184]

Those of the egalitarian persuasion point to the biblical instruction that all Christian believers, irrespective of gender, are to submit or be subject "to one another in the fear of God"[185] or "out of reverence for Christ".[186] Gilbert Bilezikian writes that in the highly debated Ephesians 5 passage, the verb "to be subject" or "to be submitted" appears in verse 21 which he describes as serving as a "hinge" between two different sections. The first section consists of verses 18–20, verse 21 is the connection between the two, and the second section consists of verses 22–33.[187]:p.153 When discussion begins at verse 22 in Ephesians 5, Paul appears to be reaffirming a chain of command principle within the family. However,

> ...when interpretation begins with verse 21, the entire passage describes mutual submission within the family. The wife submits to her husband in everything "as unto the Lord." If her husband makes a request unworthy of her Lord, her primary loyalty is "unto the Lord."... Instruction about submission is four times longer for husbands than for wives. The greatest burden of submission is clearly placed on the husband.[188]

Advocates of Christian egalitarianism believe that this model has firm biblical support:

- The word translated "help" or "helper" in Genesis 2 until quite recently was generally understood to subordinate a wife to her husband. The KJV translates it as God saying,

"I will make a help meet for him". The first distortion was extrabiblical: the noun "help" and the adjective "meet" traditionally have been combined into a new noun, "helpmate". Thus, wives were often referred to as her husband's "helpmate". Next, from the word "help" were drawn inferences of authority/subjection distinctions between men and women. "Helper" was taken to mean that husband was boss and wife his domestic. It is now realized that of the 21 times the Hebrew word 'ezer is used in the Old Testament, in eight of those instances the term clearly means "savior"—another word for Jehovah God. For example, Psalm 33 says "the Lord...is our help ('ezer) and shield". Psalm 121 reads "I lift up my eyes to the mountains—where does my help ('ezer) come from? My help ('ezer) comes from the Lord, the Maker of heaven and earth." That Hebrew word is not used in the Bible with reference to any subordinate person such a servant. [187]:p.28 Thus, forms of 'ezer in the Hebrew Bible can mean either "to save" or "to be strong" or have the idea of power and strength.[188]

- The "two becoming one" concept, first cited in Genesis 2, was quoted by Jesus in his teachings on marriage and recorded almost identically in the gospels of both Matthew and Mark. [190] In those passages Jesus reemphasized the concept by adding a divine postscript to the Genesis passage: "So, they are no longer two, but one" (NIV).

- The Apostle Paul also quoted the Genesis 2:24 passage in Ephesians 5[3] Describing it as a "profound mystery", he analogizes it to "Christ and the church".[191] Then Paul states that every husband must love his wife as he loves himself.[192]

- Jesus actually *forbids* any hierarchy of relationships in Christian relationships. All three <u>synoptic gospels</u> record virtually the same teaching of Jesus, adding to its apparent significance:[193] HYPERLINK "https://en.wikipedia.org/wiki/ Christian_views_on_marriage#cite_note-194"[194]

- The <u>Apostle Paul</u> calls on husbands and wives to be subject *to each other* out of reverence for Christ—mutual submission.[195]

- As persons, husband and wife are of equal value. There is no priority of one spouse over the other. In truth, they are one.[3] Bible scholar <u>Frank Stagg</u> and Classicist <u>Evelyn Stagg</u> write that husband-wife equality produces the most intimate, wholesome and mutually fulfilling marriages. They conclude that the Apostle Paul's statement, sometimes called the "Magna Carta of Humanity"[196] and recorded in Galatians 3, applies to all Christian relationships, including Christian marriage: "There is neither Jew nor Greek, there is neither bond nor free, there is *neither male nor female:* for you are all <u>one</u> in Christ Jesus."

- The Apostle Peter calls husbands and wives "joint heirs of the grace of life" and cautions a husband who is not considerate to his wife and does not treat her with respect that his prayers will be hindered.[197]

- Each of the six times <u>Aquila and his wife Priscilla</u> are mentioned by name in the New Testament, they are listed together. Their order of appearance alternates, with Aquila mentioned first in the first, third and fifth mentions, and Priscilla (Prisca) first in the other three.[198] Some revisions of the Bible put Priscilla first, instead of Aquila, in Acts 18:26, following the Vulgate and a few Greek texts.[199] Some scholars suggest that Priscilla was the head of the family unit.[200]

- Among spouses, it is possible to submit without love, but it is impossible to love without submitting mutually to each other.[201]

The egalitarian paradigm leaves it up to the couple to decide who is responsible for what task or function in the home. Such decisions should be made rationally and wisely,[202] not based on gender or tradition. Examples of a couple's decision logic might include:

- which spouse is *more competent* for a particular task or function;

- which has *better access* to it;

- or if they decide both are similarly competent and have comparable access, they might make the decision based on who *prefers* that function or task, or conversely, which of them *dislikes it less* than the other. The egalitarian view holds that decisions about managing family responsibilities are made rationally through cooperation and negotiation, not on the basis of tradition (e.g., "man's work" or "woman's" work), nor any other irrelevant or irrational basis.[203] HYPERLINK "https://en.wikipedia.org/wiki/Christian_views_on_marriage#cite_note-204"[204]

Complementarian view

See also: Complementarianism

Complementarians hold to a hierarchical structure between husband and wife. They believe men and women have different gender- specific roles that allow each to *complement* the other, hence the designation "Complementarians". The Complementarian view of marriage holds that while the husband

and wife are of equal worth before God, husbands and wives are given different functions and responsibilities by God that are based on gender, and that male leadership is biblically ordained so that the husband is always the senior authority figure. They state they "observe with deep concern" "accompanying distortions or neglect of the glad harmony portrayed in Scripture between the intelligent, humble leadership of redeemed husbands and the loving, willing support of that leadership by redeemed wives". [205] They believe "the Bible presents a clear chain of authority— above all authority and power is God; God is the head of Christ. Then in descending order, Christ is the head of man, man is the head of woman, and parents are the head of their children."[206] Complementarians teach that God intended men to lead their wives as "heads" of the family. Wayne Grudem, in an article that interprets the "mutual submission" of Ephesians 5 as being hierarchical, writes that it means "being considerate of one another, and caring for one another's needs, and being thoughtful of one another, and sacrificing for one another."[207]

Scriptures such as 1 Corinthians 11:3: "But I would have you know, that the head of every man is Christ; and the head of the woman is the man; and the head of Christ is God", (KJV) is understood as meaning the wife is to be subject to her husband, if not unconditionally.[208]

According to Complementarian authors John Piper, Wayne Grudem, and others, historically, but to a significantly lesser extent in most of Christianity today, the predominant position in both Catholicism and conservative Protestantism places the male as the "head" in the home and in the church.[209] HYPERLINK "https://en.wikipedia.org/ wiki/Christian_ views_on_marriage#cite_note-210"[210] HYPERLINK "https:// en.wikipedia.org/wiki/Christian_views_on_marriage#cite_ note-211"[211] HYPERLINK "https://en.wikipedia.org/wiki/

Christian_ views_on_marriage#cite_note-212"[212] They hold that women are commanded to be in subjection to male leadership, with a wife being obedient to her head (husband), based upon Old Testament precepts and principles.[213] This view holds that, "God has created men and women equal in their essential dignity and human personhood, but different and complementary in function with male headship in the home and in the Church."[214]

Grudem also acknowledges exceptions to the submission of wives to husbands where moral issues are involved.[215] Rather than unconditional obedience, Complementarian authors such as Piper and Grudem are careful to caution that a wife's submission should never cause her to "follow her husband into sin."[216]

Roman Catholic Church teaching on the role of women includes that of Pope Leo XIII in his 1880 encyclical *Arcanum* which states:

> The husband is the chief of the family and the head of the wife. The woman, because she is flesh of his flesh, and bone of his bone, must be subject to her husband and obey him; not, indeed, as a servant, but as a companion, so that her obedience shall be wanting in neither honor nor dignity. Since the husband represents Christ, and since the wife represents the Church, let there always be, both in him who commands and in her who obeys, a heaven-born love guiding both in their respective duties."[217] This position was affirmed in the 1930 encyclical *Casti Connubii*, which invokes Ephesians 5:22, "Let women be subject to their husbands as to the Lord, because the husband is the head of the wife, and Christ is the head of the Church.[218]

Though each of their churches is autonomous and self-governed, the official position of the <u>Southern Baptist Convention</u> (the largest Protestant denomination in the United States) is:

> The husband and wife are of equal worth before God, since both are created in God's image. A husband is to love his wife as Christ loved the church. He has the God-given responsibility to provide for, to protect, and to lead his family. A wife is to submit herself graciously to the servant leadership of her husband even as the church willingly submits to the headship of Christ. She, being in the image of God as is her husband and thus equal to him, has the God-given responsibility to respect her husband and to serve as his helper in managing the household and nurturing the next generation."[219]

Biblical patriarchy

<u>See also: Biblical patriarchy and Pater familias</u>

The patriarchal model of marriage is clearly the oldest one.[*according to whom?*] It characterized the theological understanding of most Old Testament writers. It mandates the supremacy, at times the ultimate domination, of the husband-father in the family. In the first century Roman Empire, in the time of Jesus, Paul, and Peter, it was the law of the land and gave the husband absolute authority over his wife, children, and slaves—even the power of life or death. It subordinates all women.

Biblical patriarchy is similar to <u>Complementarianism</u> but with differences of degree and emphasis. Biblical patriarchists carry the husband-headship model considerably further and with more militancy. While Complementarians also hold to exclusively male leadership in both the home and the church, Biblical patriarchy extends that exclusion to the civic sphere as well, so that women should not be civil leaders[220] and indeed should not have careers outside the home.[221]

Patriarchy is based on authoritarianism—complete obedience or subjection to male authority as opposed to individual freedom. Patriarchy gives preeminence to the male in essentially all matters of religion and culture. It explicitly deprives all women of social, political, and economic rights. The marriage relationship simply reinforced this dominance of women by men, providing religious, cultural, and legal structures that clearly favor patriarchy to the exclusion of even basic human dignity for wives.[158] HYPERLINK "https://en.wikipedia.org/wiki/Christian_views_on_marriage#cite_note-222"[222]

Historically in classical patriarchy, the wives and children were always legally dependent upon the father, as were the slaves and other servants. It was the way of life throughout most of the Old Testament, religiously, legally, and culturally. However, it was not unique to Hebrew thought. With only minor variations, it characterized virtually every pagan culture of that day—including all Pre-Christian doctrine and practice.[158]

While Scripture allowed this approach in Old Testament times, nowhere does the Bible ordain it. In the Hebrew nation, patriarchy seems to have evolved as an expression of male dominance and supremacy, and of a double standard that prevailed throughout much of the Old Testament. Its contemporary advocates insist that it is the only biblically valid model for marriage today. They argue that it was established at Creation, and thus is a firm, unalterable decree of God about the relative positions of men and women.[223]

Biblical patriarchists see what they describe as a crisis of this era being what they term to be a systematic attack on the "timeless truths of biblical patriarchy". They believe such an attack includes the movement to "subvert the biblical model of the family, and redefine the very meaning of fatherhood and motherhood, masculinity, femininity, and the parent and child relationship."[158] Arguing from the biblical presentation of God revealing himself "as masculine, not feminine", they believe God ordained distinct gender roles for man and woman as part of the created order. They say "Adam's headship over Eve was established at the beginning, before sin entered the world". Their view is that the male has God-given authority and mandate to direct "his" household in paths of obedience to God. They refer to man's "dominion" beginning within the home, and a man's qualification to lead and ability to lead well in the public square is based upon his prior success in *ruling his household.*[158]

Thus, William Einwechter refers to the traditional Complementarian view as "two-point Complementarianism" (male leadership in the family and church), and regards the biblical patriarchy view as "three-point" or "full" complementarianism (male leadership in family, church *and society*).[224]

The patriarchists teach that "the woman was created as a helper to her husband, as the bearer of children, and as a "keeper at home", concluding that the God-ordained and proper sphere of dominion for a wife is the household. Biblical patriarchists consider that "faithfulness to Christ requires that (Biblical patriarchy) be believed, taught, and lived". They claim that the "man is...the image and glory of God in terms of authority, while the woman is the glory of man". They teach that a wife is to be *obedient* to her "head" (husband), based upon Old Testament teachings and models.

The Jehovah HYPERLINK "https://en.wikipedia.org/wiki/ Jehovah%27s_Witnesses"' HYPERLINK "https://en.wikipedia. org/ wiki/Jehovah%27s_Witnesses"s Witnesses view marriage to be a permanent arrangement with the only possible exception being adultery. Divorce is strongly discouraged even when adultery is committed[102] since the wronged spouse is free to forgive the unfaithful one. There are provisions for a domestic separation in the event of "failure to provide for one's household" and domestic violence, or spiritual resistance on the part of a partner. Even in such situations though divorce would be considered grounds for loss of privileges in the congregation. Remarrying after death or a proper divorce is permitted. Marriage is the only situation where any type of sexual interaction is acceptable, and even then certain restrictions apply to acts such as oral and anal sex.[*citation needed*] Married persons who are known to commit such acts may in fact lose privileges in the congregation as they are supposed to be setting a good example to the congregation.[103]

Ethics and morality

All sexual relations outside marriage are grounds for expulsion if the person is not deemed repentant;[191] homosexual activity is considered a serious sin, and same-sex marriage is forbidden. Abortion is considered murder.[192] Modesty in dress and grooming is frequently emphasized. Gambling, drunkenness, illegal drugs, and tobacco use are forbidden.[193] Drinking of alcoholic beverages is permitted in moderation.[192]

The family structure is patriarchal. The husband is considered to have authority on family decisions, but is encouraged to solicit his wife's thoughts and feelings, as well as his children's. Marriages are required to be monogamous and legally registered.[194] HYPERLINK "https:// en.wikipedia.org/wiki/Jehovah%27s_

Witnesses#cite_note-199"[195] Marrying a non-believer, or endorsing such a union, is strongly discouraged and carries religious sanctions.[196] HYPERLINK "https:// en.wikipedia. org/wiki/Jehovah%27s_Witnesses#cite_note-201"[197]

Divorce is discouraged, and remarriage is forbidden unless a divorce is obtained on the grounds of adultery, which is called a "scriptural divorce".[198] If a divorce is obtained for any other reason, remarriage is considered adulterous unless the ex-spouse has died or is considered to have committed sexual immorality. [199] Extreme physical abuse, willful non-support of one's family, and what the denomination terms "absolute endangerment of spirituality" are accepted as grounds for legal separation.[200] HYPERLINK "https://en.wikipedia.org/wiki/ Jehovah%27s_ Witnesses#cite_note-205"[201]

From Wikipedia, the free encyclopedia

RIGHT DAY WRONG PERSON

In the beginning we all think that everything is "hunky Dory" and we're in love and nothing's going to change, and life will be the same with this person from day one to 30 years from now, if we even, make it that far. To find that person your, person is a blessing. It's a lot of lifelong commitment to another person other than yourself. We commit to ourselves and treat ourselves good but can we live and commit ourselves to another person to make sure that their well-being is met and cared for. As children we grow up with unconditional love. We have it no matter what we do to our parents and how we act out, or if we end up being the scholar, model child. Or the drug addict, Killer, drug dealer, prostitute. We still have that unconditional love where there are no conditions placed on us. Since when there's is an "if" in unconditional love? Unconditional love that's just it; I love you as you are good bad and ugly.

So we find that person that we've have always been looking for. We have been dating, the plan is to kiss as many of frogs we have to so that we get to the Prince as they say or the Princess. We're happy in the beginning. All our needs are met. We're able to communicate with each other we able to treat each other as equals, we are the other person's friend but somewhere along the way we end up losing that.

Now we don't know who the person is that we're lying next to. We questioned, did we even have the right person anymore we got that magical day we made it we're engaged we show everyone our ring we prepare for the wedding. We look for our wedding dress. Even the men feel good looking at tuxedos and shoes and how that day they going to look debonair haircut beard if you have one on mustache and some is even clean shaven however you look you're feeling good.

The day is near, the day has come but it taken us a long journey. Sometimes, some of us to get to that walk is it the walk of joy just for the moment? Is it the walk of a lifelong commitment and partner? Is it the walk that only lasts some a couple of months a year or two? Nowadays people don't even care about marriage. They're getting married next thing you know they wake up and want to divorce because they don't even want to try anymore. We picked that wedding day, that special day. That have some reason, significance to why we picked that day at first we can't do without that person to sometimes ending up with hating that person. Not wanting even being near that person, even in our deepest thoughts wishing that person was dead.

I don't mean that you're doing it physically, I mean it in the sense it's like you want to get rid of them so badly and sometimes you don't even know how to get rid of them sometime you lay up in the bed trying to figure out how did you get here where did I go wrong, when did that person change. The day is here, we're getting our makeup done our dress is beautiful all the ladies are ready all the men are ready. They're geared up and ready to walk down the aisle. They give their friend girlfriend the dab you done it the girls say Are you ready you say yes, I'm ready! I can't live without this person. This person is good to me. He's that person, she's the one then life happens.

We close our eyes and reflect back on the day that we did get married. The dating game when he opened up the doors talk to you nicely, took you out to dinner, took you to different places, walks in the park was even enjoyed. Everything was so romantic and you wouldn't want to be no other place than right there until now. The walk in the park is considered as being cheap and no thought put into the evening. You're just selfish. Better yet, you don't want to do anything any more. For dinners we got McDonald's or Taco Bell instead of a nice candlelight restaurant. True story not with my ex husband, but when I called myself having a boy friend He told me that he was taking me out to dinner and I got all dressed up thinking I was going somewhere nice. I told my mama and my brothers I was going on a hot date. Yeah right. So anyway I got on this red jumpsuit and my face was all made up hair done. I was ready. This fool came over and picked me up when I got in the car he said what do you want Mc Donalds or Taco Bell. I looked at him like he was crazy and I said neither, he goes on to say well we can go to tommy's and share a meal. Then he thought he was gonna take me to his house and have sex with him. I went home and told my brothers and they laughed at me, so out of line.

I just fucked up and married the wrong person because I couldn't listen to my gut and turn the other way. We ignore the red flags, He or she is going to change when we get married for the better; He is mean or she a bitch but they will change, they have just been having some bad days. No, stop it! They're who you see in front of you. Most of the time it does not get better it only gets worse because now you're in a marriage and it's not so easy to walk away now.

One should not "Marry because you can live with a person, That's just a room mate. Marry because you can't live without that person". That's a soul mate. Pray for the right person and really think about what you really want from your mate. How you really want to be treated. Look beyond that of lust and material things for all that can be lost at a blink of an eye. True love last forever and thats a blessing and grace from God. Let no one come between. No one not even some of those evil mother-in-laws. If you're lucky, not only will you gain a life long partner, you gain a new family. Mother in laws you don't lose your children to marriage you gain some extra love. Embrace them as you wanted to be accepted as well. And if you had a crazy mother- in-law, do better. I wasn't so lucky the first time around. I had an evil mother-in-law and I dealt with her for over 30 years. Now I don't have to anymore. Thank you Jesus! PS. she is probably saying the same thing about me, but Now I don't have to care anymore. When I become a mother-in-law, I vow to do better than what I had because that's a feeling I don't wish on anyone to have to endure.

STORY TIME

You know life has many cycles; we are also judge by others in a way they don't really understand why they feel that their opinion is what matters with out even being in your shoes. Some people woes are all the same just happening in a different way. Until your in my life and live my life then who are you to judge what anyone decides to take or dont. In the Bible it is quoted to say "What does judge mean in Matthew 7 1?

To judge in this way is to assume authority over others that God has not given. In the end, God will judge those who judge in this way. This does not teach that God's people should never express an understanding of the difference between right and wrong.

bibleref.com

https://www.bibleref.com   HYPERLINK   "about:blank"   › Matthew › Matthew-7-1

What does judge not lest ye be judged mean?

Judge not lest ye be judged is a powerful reminder we need today. It's a reminder to deal with our sin so that we can help those around us. It's also a warning that the harshness we use to condemn those around us will also be used to condemn ourselves. Show grace and offer correction in love.Apr 12, 2021

rethinknow.org

https://www.rethinknow.org   HYPERLINK "about:blank" ›
judge-not-what-jesus-reall..

What does Jesus say about judging?

Luke 6:37-42

37 "Do not judge, and you will not be judged. Do not condemn,
and you will not be condemned. Forgive, and you will be
forgiven. 38 Give, and it will be given to you. Given to you.

biblestudytools.com

https://www.biblestudytools.com HYPERLINK "about:blank"
› topical-verses › bible-...

Someone asks me "Do you think you're the sole cause of why
he did those things to you?" Shouldn't you blame yourself for
his actions? And not even ask me what I think just blatantly
tell me I am the cause because they would not allow those
things to happen it's my fault. Let me start out with this. first,
you can't stop people from doing what they want to do. You
have no control over anyone no matter what you think you
do. What people do when you're not around you can't control
and sometimes you can't control even if they are in your face.
I am not his or her mother and to tell the truth mothers don't
always control their children from birth they do the opposite of
what we tell them to do. We say don't do that don't touch that,
but they keep doing it anyways until they decide to stop. No
matter if they get a whooping or put on punishment, they do
it anyways. So where is the control of a person? Even if we can't

control a person as a baby how the hell do you expect to control a grown man or women?

So why should you place blame on me when we can't control anyone actions. I am not accountable for what someone else choose to do. Good or bad. We all come here by ourselves and the smart one's in the back who says we are twins etc. you still come into the world one at a time. You are an individual your own ways own mind. And when we die, we die by ourselves and are judged by God on our own deeds not together.

So, no I don't blame myself for the choices he decided to do on his own. We all know right from wrong even if we are not taught that from our parents as we grow it is in us to know right from wrong and what's well and what is bad.

People are so eager to tell you my man or women wouldn't do this or that too me. Ha, I have news for you, they most of the time are doing just what you said they would not do it just haven't gotten back to you yet. Trust God it will and then you come back and tell me again what someone want to do to you. I don't care how pretty you are, sexy, good Pussy, money all that doesn't matter even ugly people get cheated on or disrespected at some point.

Being married don't stop things from happening it just make you have someone to go though things with so you're not alone. Key word is you're not alone. No one wants to be alone. Even if we lie to ourselves and say I am good being alone that is only good for a little while, because we are not made to live alone. We need to be loved and cared for.

What I take you could not take and what you take I couldn't take why? Because it's not meant for us to go threw the things that is not meat at the time for us. Not to say we will never cross the same path we will just have different timing.

Now I went threw a lot of mental abuse never physical, but a lot of people go thew the physical, or both. I feel like the mental is worse because it's embedded into your mind. Bruises you can recover from, so I was told. But I really don't believe that cause some burses leaves scars as well. All of it is wrong no matter how it is given and taken. When you see a couple that has been married a long time and I am not talking just a few years were talking about 15 years plus you best to believe they have endured a lot of stuff they're too embarrassed to tell anyone even family for fear of judgement.

I didn't have to tell my own embarrassment mine did it right in front of everyone even when it was behind my back everyone else knew before I did. It was some that even helped or said it was okay.

My husband had family members on his side tell him like example: if he was out of town, they would say stuff like "Dog it's okay to mess around on your wife not girlfriend but wife if your out of state she won't know get yours". And most of the time it was with people they knew. Watch out for those devils because they will help you fuck up what is good because sometimes, they don't like their situation. Low key jealous. See they see what is projected not the reality of what really goes down at home. Life you see what people want you to see not as how they truly are.

People can have it all in front of people but when they get home or alone where no one is watching may not even be talking to each other or worse no sex or kisses, but you see the joy.

I remember once my ex had pictures posted on his page with his whore and I said you look happy, and she had him to post and sometimes it would be her posting not him just to get back at me to show me how supposedly happy they were. Jokes on her he wasn't happy, and I still talked to him every day. Side note he still was my best friend even throw he was with that whore but was he really? Yeah nope. See what you do to others will come back to you. And best to believe it did. I would have sex with him just because I knew I could. And I wasn't going to let her get away with her messing with my husband and I didn't mess with her boyfriend. He never remarried. So, every time I wanted to have sex with him, I did because I knew I could and besides he was my husband. and the get back was real. She thought he wasn't going to do her the way he did me. HA HA the joke was on her this time.

She really didn't trust him even when he was away from me, and he was out of state with her. Because this whore wanted to place a tracking device on his car, so she knew where he was. Crazy how people don't have a problem sneaking around with someone else's man/ women, husband / wife but oh no you not going to do them that way. Stupid. Well, I had sex with him for my own needs and devious intentions. Mind you I did it when I wanted to not when he wanted to, I didn't have anyone and I want my needs met and it was safer then going to get some random dude. And he was the only guy I had for over 30 years. So that was that co dependency thing again.

A lot of the time most people go back and get some from their baby mama we don't want to believe they will but if given the opportunity it will happen because it easy, they will always have that connection. Now it doesn't mean everyone will, but it does happen so never say never.

Story: one day when I was dating my husband, he had a baby mama, and I was working and one day he dropped me off to work in my car no doubt and he went off about his day doing what ever and so long story short he left me at work. I ended up staying at work over night. He never came and got me. I waited and waited, and he never came until it was time for me to get off the next day. The embarrassment of it all so I spent the night at my desk. So, when everyone came in, I pretended that I just came in early for overtime when I really was left at work. So, when he picked me up, he just said oh I am sorry bae I went to go see my daughter and My baby mama (he said her name) locked me inside the house and left me there and I had no way to get out. You know and I know that was a lie. At that time, I didn't say nothing just went home. I was tired of crying.

My point is we go threw a lot behind closed doors that no one knows about. We don't tell. Any way back to the pictures on Facebook the joy of it all. Well, I would say to him I see your soooo very happy, you have a gang of pictures of you and your whore and yes, every time I spoke to him about her, she was a whore or bitch. That was her name. she made sure that they were blasted all over so I could see how soo happy they were. Lol. Anyway, he would tell me just because you see me smiling doesn't mean I am happy that is just a picture for show. They would just be in the car having an argument on they way to a party at friend's house and not even talking to each other and then soon as they get in front of other people act like they were so in love. So, what you see is not always the reality of what's really going on.

I stayed and took a lot because I loved my husband and love is an emotion that has no timing. When your tired of someone you will let go but its not in other people's time but your own and God's timing. All you can do is give advice its up to the other person when to leave or stay. Just hope you leave before something bad happens. Side note: be careful when it's the matter of the heart because you will end up being the hater when all you were doing is trying to help or cared. Unless it's physical just step back and wait till they come to you for help just never give up on them because we all need someone to care and not give up on us even when we have given up on ourselves.

LIVING WITHOUT SEX

W hen we first fall in love all we do is have sexual tension. We can't get enough of each other just want to do it anywhere and everywhere. When you get married and real life steps in and you start having kids and the sex goes from everyday, 3 times a day, to 3 days a week if you're lucky, to once a month. And sometimes none at all. You forget to even have sex. Sometimes you get so busy and tired that you don't even remember if you had any. Then that's when the problems start.

So you know that as we get older the sex changes for everyone. What you liked when you first got married or when you were younger, you don't like anymore. In marriage, one partner may have evolved and want to try new things and the other partner may be okay with the same stuff that now bore you to death.

Sometimes it even comes to the point that your love making seems more like a chore than pleasure. You be like 'shit, he or she wants to do it and you're like I hope this don't take to long.' Even though I would enjoy it just didn't want too sometimes.

Sometimes as the years pass, you say come on let's get this over with. You start praying please let him hurry and not make this long. Or you fake that you had an orgasm so they would get off of you.

We used to want to satisfy our partners, but when they make us mad and still want to have sex you no longer care. The children are born and you're tired. Better yet, some men don't want to have oral sex with the wife once she has had the kids or pregnant. Let's keep it real, if your man had a small penis you would lie to him and say it was big just to pump up his ego. As the years pass you get into an argument you call his penis little. Now you don't care about his feelings. Men where you use to slap that ass and say 'this is some good ass pussy' you no longer think it's good anymore now it's loose and worn out. You forgot that you're the one that gotten it that way from all the time you were having sex in the beginning. Now you want some younger or new pussy. Note: all vagina snap back. And younger females have more surgery on their vagina than older women or women that have has children.

You have peer pressure that say 'hey you still hitting that old stuff.' (I don't mean old women I mean same girl) 'when you gonna get some new pussy.' 'Man you missing out!' But what are you really missing out on? Nothing. We have to ask ourselves what made it good in the first place? What changed? Why I don't want to try to make my partner feel good anymore? Why my baby is out of shape now and I don't find them sexually appealing anymore yet I go get someone else out of shape or bigger.

No matter what, we find an excuse instead of fixing it. We are much more happier when we have sex, and sex is needed for our health. We find it easier to get someone else rather than to tell our partner's what we want and need in the bedroom. Worse, we get churchified and think that we no longer can have sex. Hello,

Church people have sex too!!! They are some undercover freaks. They won't admit it but ask the Deacon or the Pastor that's getting it in more than you with "Sister Jones." Women you go to church and act like now you cant have sex anymore. You use to watch porn to learn new tricks. Now you just lay there or the men just bam bam bam and think they did something when you just not hitting the spot.

Communication is lost when we change as we get older, or more in years of marriage. What I liked before I don't want you to do and you think I like it cause I let you do it. I only did that cause you thought you was doing something now we're married, I don't like it. Many have secret fantansies and the other partner doesn't know because you're too afraid to tell, fearing you will be judged. So you get someone else to fill that part of you're needs. Now your partner finds out you're heading to divorced court cause you no longer think that person is any good in bed. Note: most of the time what you like to do your partner does to you just never asked.

People get divorced because of bad sex. And is it really bad sex or you're just bored and you use that as an excuse. Many want to add new partners to feel like that's whats missing. And the other goes along just to keep the other happy. If you go into more of a spiritual sex, you will feel good even with the old. Note: all new is not always better. Mr. 'swing a ling' comes along and give her some attention, she's gone! I used to want sex outside, when I got older nope we not doing that but when we was dating we did it anywhere. When you want out of the marriage, you find things in sex to use so that it's one of the reason you want to leave. Sad part is you will get with the new one and do all those things I ask for you to do and go do it with them.

I asked one time to be placed up against the wall and he said that would hurt his back. But I see big girls getting picked up all the time by a skinny dude. Yet when you playing 'stud muffin,' you tossing them in the air like a frisbee. When do we stop trying to make the other feel good? Some people use sex to get the ring, the house, the car. New body; yeah I went there. Then after all that we no longer think the sex is good. And now we want out when it really wasn't good in the first place. You just had a need to fill. We used to want to have oral sex all the time now it's yuckie.

We turn away from sex sometimes. We start using criticism, belittling, or slurs toward our man's manhood, and men do the same about the experience of his woman or her body parts. Example: it smells down there. Instead of telling her to go get checked he just stop having sex.

What happens if you can't have sex anymore? Now you want to leave Excuse now we have plenty of toys some feel so real. And Women all we have to do is open up, you can always get it. But we have something else to use to get out of this relationship. Story time:

Once there was a couple that got married and the husband was more into freaky stuff than the wife. When they were dating, he never told her that he needed extra women to keep him happy until 5 years later he wanted to become a swinger 'cause he was tired of just her. I consider that just an open way to cheating. Most women do it for the guy, to keep him happy so that he won't leave but you never said that is what you wanted from the start. Now if you don't, I will find someone that will. We are now not on the same page. Men sometimes feel that if they get someone younger that she is tighter, that's not the case most of the time. Younger females have more sex sometimes than older women. They can be 20 had 30 partner cause all the guys think she fresh but the older lady has only had 4 or 5. Just 'cause she's older doesn't mean she's loose. Some also think that after you have a baby, the sex drive ends. It's more mental. Not that she can't. Find out what's wrong.

We find many excuses to say the sex is no good so we can leave when we want out. But that comes with the marriage we sometimes like it sometimes we don't. But that part of real life. We don't want the real life. We want only the fantasy.

Psychology Today estimates that roughly **15 to 20 percent** of American marriages are sexless, not counting the over 50 percent of unions that end in divorce. That 15 to 20 percent of married couples are living without sex, 'lonely and longing for real love, and the opportunity to express that love through sexual intimacy.'

Infidelity in the United States is said to be responsible for 20-40% of divorces. This is a finding by the American Psychological Association. Furthermore, there are several sources of data on the link between cheating and divorce. According to a study conducted by Georgia University, almost a fifth of married couples didn't have sex in the 12 months preceding the said study. Roughly 27% of women and 15% of men did not have sex in the last 12 months, according to an article published in VeryWellMind. 7.

No sex in a relationship is really a gateway to other problems. Some can be medically induced. Some men feel if their wives have a hystorestomy that she don't feel the same anymore. (This is not true! Just wanted to put that out there.) Many are not willing to work on finding out the why's and either live in a sexless marriage or leave for the most part they leave because they find it more easier to do because they really want out.

Some people stop wanting to have sex with their partner because of cheating. Everything I would find out my husband cheated on me I wouldn't have sex with him for a long time. I wanted no part of him or the other person. That's nasty. Especially if I knew them. Most of the time I did know them. And the type of men they would have sex with and how loose they was with giving it away. Some even had STD's.

Sad too say been there. I remember a time when my husband was with this girl and his friends was like man talk to her so I could talk to her friends and he did. One day a couple of his friends and a family member came over and told him to come with them that the girl my husband was seeing was gonna take them all shopping so he went and stayed 3 days in that three days it was really hard for me I had 3 kids and they all was small I was going to the store with no car and had one baby in the front and one inside the basket and one holding on too the basket. We lived on the third floor in our apartment. I had to bring the basket into the lobby leave my groceries and go take the kids into the house at the same time praying no one would steal my food. And also nothing should happen to my babies while I would go get the food.

Anyway we went two days not hearing from him and so I found out where he was and me and my friends went over to the girls house. They was all in her apartment partying you could here them all the way down stairs. So I found the girls car and tore it up. I broke every window and sliced every tire. She couldn't go no where in that car. You wanted to take everybody shopping now go buy a new car bitch I said too myself.

Well three days past and he came home the day before Thanksgiving I will never forget and had Hickie's all over his neck. She did on purpose cause she knew he was going home. She asked him if he wanted her to drop him off he said no he took the bus. I knew cause I ask how he got home. So any who We had sex that night. Don't judge me I loved my husband and he was mine I could have sex with him if I wanted too. So the next day we went to my grandmother's house for Thanksgiving dinner and mind you all the Hickie's on his neck. Well we got there and everyone thought I did it and everything someone would reference it he would hold my hand tighter cause I didn't tell them I didn't put them there. No one didn't even know he was gone for three days. My family knew nothing. Some of his did cause they was with him.

So when we got back home the next day he says to me babe I have to tell you something I said what is it I thought he was gonna leave me. He said I am burning I said what that means? He said I think I got something. I slapped him not knowing if he was gonna hit me back. And he didn't he took the slap. We went too the doctor sure nuff he had an STD. And so did I we both got shots. I once asked him why her he said she only loves me. I said What about me I only love you. Yet I wasn't the one who gave you STD but she only loving you I said too him looks like she loving on more than just you.

When we got our shots the doctor told him he was stupid for having a wife and having to bring me to the clinic to get medicine for what he has done.

So this was why a lot of the times when I found out or even heard he was messing with someone I wouldn't have him for a while at least when he wanted it. I would only do it when I wanted it.

Yes I forgave him. And yes I stayed married for 20 more years after that.

CAT FISH

Let's start here. EVERYONE GET'S CAT FISHED! There are no exceptions to this rule. When we meet someone for the first time, we are catfishing. When we date we're cat fishing. When we get married, we're cat fishing. We're always cat fishing at some point. You sometimes never know who a person really is until you been with them for a while. Some live a double life and so you don't know who or what you're really getting. Sadly, it happens to us all.

The dating apps. You go to the apps and put your profile in and you try to do your best so they can see the good in you, 'cause if you sometimes show the true you, they may not like you so 'let's make up some things so I can get a date.' Maybe even get laid for the night. Let's take a picture so I can show my naked face. Nope! I have filters, makeup. Filters and make-up whoop some of us need to sleep with the make-up on thank goodness for makeup. You are cat fishing cause half the people don't look the same when they take off the makeup. We don't have no teeth, spots on our face. Bags, rings around the eyes, but with makeup we can make magic. Put that magic wand on us now we're breathtaking.

Thats what we want people to see. I once met this guy that married this lady, he thought she was so beautiful and one day she got caught with no makeup on and he divorced her. Why?

because he said that she was not the woman he married. Why was that? Because she cat fished him. He never saw her without make up. She would always go to bed looking amazing and wake up before he did and put on a fresh face. So, one day he came home to surprise her and she wasn't ready and there she was bare faced. And he screamed. He said, "who are you?" She said "your wife." "The hell you are," he replied. "Yes, honey it's me." But I never seen you like this. I know I always wanted to look beautiful for you." "But you're a lie. You don't even look like the person I married not even a little bit."

Come to find out, it takes her 2 hours or more to put on her face that her husband came to love. But she was too ugly for him. He wanted the trophy wife that he married. She said "no one will see me like this but you." He said "I don't want to even see you." Now the heart just went out the door. "But baby I love you," he goes on to say "but I love the person you showed me."

She replied "I am the same person. He said, "no you're not. You are not who I married. So much for love." He divorced her and got it because she gave him an illusion of someone else. When we use body shapers, we give the illusion because our stomachs are not really flat. We feel better. Nothing is wrong with the illusion if the other person knows the truth. The unknown is what hurts.

When we get a new boyfriend/girlfriend, we start off nice and loving each other. Say the most wonderful things to each other. We can't get enough of each other. After a while then the real "you" comes out sooner or later. Many people let you know the "real" them within 3 months or less. Some are really good in not letting you know the "real" them until after the marriage. As well as many years living a double life. Many will lead you to believe that they are God fearing and gentle, kind but not at all.

Some will use God to get to know someone, because they know you love Jesus and that's how they can get to you.

Many will quote scriptures to make you think they're really are into the word. Pastors will preach today loving on someone's wife, or cheating on their wife or husbands. All in the name of Jesus. I mean it gets bad. They lie so hard till you believe them. They believe themselves. The lie becomes the truth. Until you find out. God is watching us. I can't lie to you or hurt you. What would I get out of it? I want a wife. I prayed for you and God answered my prayers. God put us together. Most of the time, God didn't put you with that person. He did give you warning signs and you chose to ignore them.

But you can't help yourself because you want love. What do you do? They make you feel so good. You haven't felt this way in years. Your heart is full of joy, and on top of this, he love's Jesus! So that makes him the one. Not always true. The devil has many faces, shapes, and personalities.

Married life: You get through the wedding, now real-life!

Steps in hopefully you haven't been dating long. I say this because I believe within 6 months of dating, a man know if it's you, he wants to make his wife. I feel sorry for women that wait years and years to get married. Because at this point, even with him being with you, he was still searching. He's keeping his options open just in case someone else comes along that he feels maybe better. Not always true. You can miss your blessing by searching for someone else while he/she is right beside you.

After years, most of the time they go ahead and get married because you left them no other choice but to do so. Circumstances! If you don't marry me, I will leave! Someone becomes ill and really need someone to care for them. And they know that you're the only one that will make sure they are okay. Something that the new man, or woman won't do. For example, let's not be able to have sex anymore, the new side piece isn't here for all that. You're not any fun anymore. They're out!

The vows you made when you got married, first the Lie. Here comes the cat fish! You said for sickness and in health. Okay, I am really here mostly for the good health part. The sickness, I will sometimes try to tolerate. You get sick there is no more focus on you. Your spouse needs all the attention. Some just can't and won't live up to the part of sickness. Let's be honest, we will find a reason to get out. You lied! I married you for in sickness and health. You said yes!

To death do us part. a lot of people say to hell with that. I am not speaking on the abusers, let the record reflect I am speaking on the norm. You have a bad attitude, you're a cheater, you lose your job, the sex no good anymore, you can't have kids, you won't let me have another partner plus you. People fine the simplest things to get out of what they had promised. So, you cat fished me, because you said you was going to be and do all these things you lead me to believe you.

The double life, the side piece, the other whole family, the serial killer, the robber, the thief, the rapist. All this is part of cat fishing. We didn't know about none of these things. Because if we did, we would probably not be with you. The side piece. Sometime we know that the other person is taken sometimes we don't.

When you're the side piece and you know who your dating has someone else, he is cat fishing you because most of the time that person leads you to believe that you are better than what he / she has at home.

They make you feel extra special. Tell you that you're amazing, you're better than what they have at home. Whatever you want to hear, you got it coming. Then they go home and say the same thing to their spouse. So now both of you are getting cat-fished. The side piece led you to believe that they would do anything for you if you were their's fully. That's a lie. Most of the time they don't want you to really be their's fully because that is too much responsibility. As soon as you leave, they're happy 'cause you go home and you just gave them what they needed and now they have a sense of worth.

For the most part, the side piece is gaslighting too, 'cause if you finally leave and come to them all things change. The real them comes out and sometimes you don't even like that person.

Because that person was only good to you when you were sneaking. Once my husband had told me that he had this side person. I say this to be nice and said oh she loves me. I said What about me? I love you too. Yeah, but she only wants me. And she makes me feel good. She doing for me what I want her to do and she only wants me. Here's the kicker. One weekend he left and went out with his friends and didn't come home for the whole weekend. And no one in my family knew. But his friends and brother knew. One of his friends would say "man just talk to her so I can talk to the friend."

So, he did. This went on for a while. One day, she told him to come over him and his friends. His friends were dating her friends so she promised to take them all shopping so they all went. Long story short, he was gone three days. And came home on the day before Thanksgiving. Me being happy that he was home. He came in with ickie's all around his neck, but I ignored them, still just happy he was home.

We had SEX. (judge me if you want, I don't care.) That was my husband. So anyway, we went to my grandmother's house for Thanksgiving, and when we got there, they started teasing us saying because he had hickie's all over his neck that "we know what you guys been doing, don't be making no more babies" LOL.

Knowing that I didn't put those hickie's on his neck, he just grabbed my hand and stroked them knowing that I wasn't going to tell the truth. I just smiled and sucked it up. The next day it was when I came home, he said Vetta I have something to tell you and he had this look on his face. I knew something was wrong. In my head he was leaving again. This time for good. Not the case this time. So, I said "what?" I didn't sit down. He said "I am burning" I said what that means. He went on to say I got something I need to go to the doctor. For the first time I slapped him.

I didn't know if he was going to hit me back or not at that time, I didn't care. For the record he NEVER hit me the whole time we were married. Anyway, I said to him "she only loved you though, right? She only made you feel good right? Looks like to me she was making someone else feel good too." So, the next day we went to the doctor's office and we both got medical shots to cure the STD we both now had.

One thing I liked about the visit was the doctor asked him about all the people he had had sexual relations with, and then ask him who was I to him. He said "my wife." He then told him that he was stupid and a damn fool. From my knowledge he never saw that person again. Oh Yeah so you know when he was gone them days I found out where the girl stayed and me and my friends mostly me, I tore up that girl's car so that she couldn't go to work. Since I felt she wanted to pay for stuff, now you can pay for this.

I was young but I sliced up all her tires, and busted out all her windows. She needed a new car, when I was done. That was so wrong of me but felt so right and it felt soooo much better than sex. His friends came to me and said We know you did it. I said "did you see me? Nope, then it wasn't me." HAHA.

Moving forward. The dating app Swindler. Many people now use the dating sights to find their soulmate, sex mates. Well that's where the real cat fishes come from. Since Covid, we were all inside and that was really the only new way to meet people was online. We all know about that so I will just tell you about my Cat Fish. I got Cat Fished by the same person twice. Sounds crazy but true. So, this guy found me on social media, and started dming me. I went to his page and found that he was supposed to be in the service, and very handsome.

So okay now it's a maybe. He has some interiority and a job all that. Now I haven't dated since I had gotten divorced so I was ready after 6 years. I felt it was time to let someone in. At the time I was in a dark place. I was lonely. I had just lost the man, my ex-husband (he passed away), my kids' father, the man I loved half my life. Here comes this man saying all the things I needed to hear. He made me feel wanted. And loved. Wow, someone loves me, wants only me. I don't have to share anymore. He told me I was the answer to his prays. A lot went on in-between so moving forward, I was supposed to marry this man. I fell hard. 90-day fiancée, I was ready! Married at first sight.

All that was us. So anyway, we only were texting nothing else. So, it was getting time for him to come visit and then he asked for money to help him get here from Paris. Stupid me, I sent the plane ticket money and then some extra. Paid for a room for him to stay. He didn't show up. So, I didn't hear from this guy for 3 months. Anyway, I call Cat Fish the show, because I wanted for find out who I was talking to for almost a year and he took my money. I wanted it back.

So anyway, I didn't wait for them to contact me. I went on to find him myself. So, I found the real guy of the pictures that I had. So, I wanted to let him know that there's a guy out here pretending to be him. Dude had a different name but the same last name and pictures. Here the double. So, I ended up talking to the new guy.

As the days and months went by, I fell deeper for this guy not knowing that he possibly could be the same man who cat fished me before. So, as the months went on, he started saying the same things that the other guy would say. Acting the same way. So, I would say "you sound just like the other guy" and he would get mad saying that I am not him. But I caught him saying the exact same thing the other guy said verbatim. I said that "You are the same guy. OMG You lied." He was trying to get me again. But I was smarter this time. You may get me once; I promise you won't get me twice.

I will keep you posted as to what happen next. But please everyone be careful who you talk to online. Everyone is not honest and anyone can be Cat-Fished. But you can also find true love. I found mine. My "love under new management" as Miki Howard would say. I so love this man! And this time I feel like I found a man just for me. A man who I don't have to share or be afraid to love. Update: So my catfish dude ended up showing his true face and really wanting me. Realizing that he lost a phenomenal woman. And he wasn't ugly, so I don't know why he pretended to be someone else. But he missed his blessing with me.

My Fantasy Is Not My Reality

When we are younger we all thank of that fairy tale romance and all will be happily ever after but this is not the case the real reality is nothing is happily ever after everything is conjured up in our heads of what we would want our life to be there we are disappointed when reality really sets in we meet the guy we fall in love, we dated for a little while and then we get married have kids and sometimes that don't even happen in that order but the reality is marriage takes a lot of work and time to get it right because of the simple fact that you're putting together two different lives two different people two different DNA's no one is the carbon copy of yourself but we try to make those people be we try to make them be what we want to be we just say and set out to say that we will love them if only if they were more like me or if they would do as we say or want them to do well in reality individuals are never the same and when you put that together in a marriage we realized that marriage is way more harder than we expected to be life throws us challenges life takes us on different journeys one grows the other stays no one needs have changed one have not we sometimes outgrow the things that we accepted in the past now is not included in our future.

When we try to understand the other person we say I can change that person it's just you know I just got to take time and work on them they are conformed to what I want them to be that when and when the truth is you can't change a person that don't want to be changed and that person was made perfect in God's eyes who are you to try to change something that God made perfect because in his eyes when he created that person the prayers person was created in his image and that person's soul is exactly the way God meant for him to be so who are we to try to change somebody or think that we can when in actuality we can't.

The definition of a "soul" in the bible a soul is your makeup your personality who you are what you represent that's what your soul is the "Soul designates the whole person as characterized by desires, wishes, even craving. Emphasizing that human are emotional beings. According to <u>Genesis 2:7</u> God did not make a body and put a soul into it like a letter into an envelope of dust; rather he formed man's body from the dust, then, by breathing divine breath into it, he made the body of dust live, i.e. the dust did not *embody* a soul, but it *became* a soul – a whole creature.[8]

We get into relationships thinking that we don't like all the things about a person but when we get them married to us we can mold them into who we want them to be. By the way that never works. We try to conform ourselves to be what someone else vision of who we should be for them then we become unhappy. After so long we then want out or someone else comes along as love us for who we are. Then comes the divorce. Now your pissed because all the effort you put into trying to change that person didn't work out for you. You knew they was going to be what you wanted them to be the transition was almost there. They didn't follow through with your plan. Remember your plan is different from theirs. They are not you. You are two different people with different mindsets and goals.

Our expectations on what marriage looks like or what we saw when we grew up is not what we live like now. My mom and dad stayed married 301 years but yours only lasted a year maybe 7 if you're lucky. Why is that so? Back in the day women were more submissive to their husband. Not now. Women want to be in control and men are allowing it because if you want to be the man in this, then you take it on. Less things for me to worry about since you feel that you could do a better job than the man. So now the man is allowing you to take that role but that's not what God had planned that why a lot of marriages doesn't work because you didn't follow the plan, God's plan! not yours. Silly women and shame on the man who allows us to take over this role because they don't want to have the responsibility of being just that, The Man.

Have you notice the structure of a man's body? compared to that of the women? Lets examine this for a minute. The mans form is solid and strong full of muscle hardly any fat. If he is fat most of the time, its because he is lazy and complacent. IE the gamer. When a man does get fat it takes him no time to get his body in shape because he was not built to be fat or hold on to it. A man was built on strength, to be able to hunt and work to provide for his family. A man was built totally different than that of his woman. The structure of the woman body is different from that of our Kings. We hold lots of fat, everything mostly on us is fat. It's hard for us to lose fat because it is supposed to be there. We are the bearers of the children we are the nurturer we are to feed the babies we was not built to work the fields that why we tire quicker then that of a man. It takes us months to years to lose the weight that it takes a man a month to lose. Why is that? God's plan the man is the leader. The provider, the head even his feet is tougher then ours so why do we feel that we can change the plan. When we do it never works. We as women at the end not happy because it becomes too much for us. Sometimes. Not saying bow down and be a stepping stone. That was not the plan either. The plan was to be the helper, have our men back when they fall short. Not to make them feel inadequate or not worthy of. That's when eventually they go looking for someone else to replace you. And you thought that you couldn't be replaced. Ya okay keep thinking that. The court house is full of women that thought just like you.

So you got him to the wedding of your dreams, now what? Play time over now. Now no more pretending no more yes sir, yes ma'am now it's "oh hell no" and "you're crazy" and now where we didn't argue about certain subjects we are now. I thought you were this way now you have changed. No, they didn't change, you just missed it. Remember in your head you thought you could change that person. They catfished you real good. Your expectations was totally different then what they had planned. The man she catfished you too, hello you had this super sweet woman that only showed that side of her and as my ex called it, "she got the sweeties personality." Yeah that lasted just as long as it took for me to let go and he went to her to learn that her personality was really messed up. He no longer know the woman that did anything to try to break up his marriage when he was with her and didn't have to sneak around anymore he didn't even like her anymore. The real person emerge.

Suga' Daddies, yeah they pay for love when all they have to do is really tell their wife what they like you know if you tell us those things you just might find out we like the same things as you do. Communication folks that the key. You men think that women don't like freaky sex. You would be amazed of what we like to do. Or you think you have to find you a younger girl to do those things. Alert! We like that freaky stuff too! When you don't do it, we get men that will do it just like you do. We go seek out that man to blow our back out.

I used to ask my husband who considered him self in shape to pick me up against the wall and let have sex he would say oh my back. Can't do that. Made me feel like I was too fat for him to lift. But he would brag that he could lift over 200 lbs, I wasn't even that heavy. But I would see other guys that was smaller in stature and pick up women bigger then I was do it. So that what I look for now. I ask can you do this and if he give me that same excuse your not for me. Keep it pushing. I need to be tossed up and flipped around and all that stuff you thinking you can only get from a younger girl. You try so hard with them sweating and out of breath trying to keep up but get home and tired and cant do nothing. Men open your eyes. We're getting it in too while your searching for that outside fix. By the way, she is only with you for the payday. She doesn't even like you. And nor does she want to be with you when real life stuff happens. The clean up man is waiting for us. And they are putting in work and not just by sex either for the shallow people in the back.

Everyone wants the easy way out. If it doesn't work lets get a divorce. I don't want to try its too hard it was supposed to be easy. It was good in the beginning, now look at us. Here comes the kids. I no longer have the shape I had a couple of years ago nor do you sometimes but I am judged more harshly. I can't work. I can't give you kids that you wanted. I got hurt and unable to do my duties as a spouse. I just didn't live up to your expectations that you had for us. Your plan. No matter what we have planned you may notice a lot of the time that was not lined up with God's plans for us. But when things get hard its easier to bail out and start over for the fun times then to work on the passing time. All bad times never last but we don't want to go through the bad times, we want it to stay in the meantime. What if he loses his job, will you stay? Some do, some don't. A man being a provider will say if his woman loses her job, I got you baby. I am the provider but what happens if he could no longer provide? We make the mistake of making him feel less than a man. He already feels less then a man because now he has a broken promise that he made to you. The pressure is on. Now he is a low life good for nothing all the bad things in the world but before he was everything.

You took that vow for richer or poorer. You really didn't mean that. You was just saying that because that's what the vows say. Now people don't even fake it they say for richer or richer listen they are telling you if you go poor I am out, period! Then they laugh when they say it but they really mean it. So don't be surprised when they leave because they told you so. Reality is that you are taking two different people and making them as one learning their ways that mostly have been hidden until after the wedding. Now the make up comes off. And you see the real person. No more faking liking the food you cook, the way you clean, the clothes you wear the lax in wanting to have goals and the free spirit that just want to look at life as live for now worry about what going to happen in the future later. It wasn't a issue on who made the most money. Or if one is excelling and the other is not. What was tolerated is no longer. One used to drink now you can't be controlled. One wants to hang out with friends all the time, party all the time and the other one is too tired to go or just want to be with you where that was good enough now it not. We used to shop now we don't as often because now we have higher bills. All life changing things that happen right when you get married. The very next day after the wedding. That's why no one is wanting to get married now they use the excuse of it's just a piece of paper we don't need that baby. Lie we tell. Also if you haven't gotten married after 2 years note he or she is still looking for that right one. It doesn't take you 6 or more years to know if your marriage material. That's why we get mad after we have put in so many years and then you break up for the next person to be with them less then a year and they get married. Now we question what was wrong with me. The answer is you was not the right person.

DECIDING TO SAY GOODBYE

Deuteronomy 24:1 (KJV) When a man hath taken a wife, and married her, and it come to pass that she find no favor in his eyes, because he hath found some uncleanness in her: then let him write her a bill of divorcement, and give it in her hand, and send her out of his house.

Deuteronomy 24:2 (KJV) And when she is departed out of his house, she may go and be another man's wife.

These two scriptures goes for both men and women.

It was not til I divorced I would look for another man to fill the voids that was missing in my marriage. See My biggest fear was not of losing my husband but of losing God's grace. I didn't want God to be mad at me for taking a vow with him and not holding up to my promises. I also had children.

Coming from a broken family, I didn't want that for my kids. I wanted them to have their father at home, at all cost. And it cost me a lot until most of them were grown and I didn't want to take it anymore.

Once I felt I still would have God's grace, I decided to leave. And the only way I felt I could make it count or hurt him in some way was leaving and divorcing him. See most cheaters don't care much if you cheat on them. They "chalk" it up to the game. Well if she cheated on me, so what I did it a lot of times. So I can forgive her or him for that matter. So knowing that, the worse thing to do is leave especially when they think that no matter what they do you're not going to leave them.

My husband's family would tell him "you can do what ever, she not going anywhere." Thinking like I had all these kids would discourage men from wanting me or that's thinking he was the best I could get. None of which was true. But people have their own perceptions of what it was. I wanted to hurt him in some way finally for all the times he hurt me.

The hardest thing to do for me was the only and best thing that would hurt him the most. Me leaving. Took me over 30 years to do so but I finally did it with no regrets. After he passed away, I second guessed myself. But before that, we were best friends all was forgiven and I moved on. Well, he moved on he did. I never did, until now kind of. Because I have no other choice. I don't want to be alone.

I have already felt alone long enough when I was married. I didn't just stay in my marriage just so the kids could have their father. I stayed because no matter what, I loved my husband and I lived up too my vows even if he didn't. I still love him but I knew I had to go. I deserved better.

After many years of people telling me what they did with my husband and how good he made them feel or they just wanted to have sex with him just too see if they could or if he was good or not. The whore's was mostly people I knew. That's the sad part. It would be people that I had dealings with, close friends, well people I thought were my friends. They knew he was married but that didn't stop them from trying or doing it. One girl would tell me she didn't care about him being with other women because he didn't belong to her, he belongs to me. One I found out said she just wanted to give him head. Or wanted him to do her to see if he was good at it.

I couldn't take it anymore. It had been way pass time to time to go. What did I have too lose? Nothing! We had no assets, the kids was all almost grown. I took ME back! As hard as I fought for my marriage, the more I had against me including family. His family. And when you have a mom that doesn't honor your marriage that makes it worse. But that's in the next book. "When hell comes in the form of a mother's In-law."

Many say you don't love yourself or you allowed it. Even they would say worse, "you taught him to treat you that way." Bullshit to all of it. I stayed 'cause I loved him and you can't make anyone do what they don't want too.

God gave us free will therefore he could do what he wanted. In the end, it will be between him and God. Everyone is accountable for their own sin just 'cause it say when you get married you become one. But doesn't mean you take on their sin also when you are born, you came by yourself, you die by yourself and God judgements is also done individually.

So all I had to worry about was myself. Not him, but me. So with every choice made, there are also consequences. My choice was to leave the marriage. The result was sometimes loneliness, not having someone to come home too. Not having someone to love. But the good part was I gained myself back. Not being embarrassed, not hurting, no more tears, not feeling ashamed, and no one talking behind my back or other people knowing who my husband was having an affair with.

The worse hurt is hanging with people your husband is having an affair with. And not knowing. But they're judgments are coming too. I believe in Karma. She finds you no matter where you are. But I am happy I decided to leave because I never wanted my kids to think that this was okay.

So when dealing with deciding to leave let it be your choice, know your not alone, listen to your spirit you don't have to hurt that way. Pray for strength and guidance. And smile letting go sometimes is hard but is sometimes the best thing for you to do.

Know that sometimes all things are not permanent some get remarried when they see what was lost was worth more then The temporary satisfaction. And we also have to look at what we could have done better. It's not always one person s fault.

But that's where communication comes in. If your not happy about something in your relationship let the other person know so they can try to fix it. Because sometimes things can be fixed when you know there is a problem. No one is a mind reader you have to speak up or lose what you once loved.

Now that he is gone I do realize that I could have done somethings different or better in my marriage. But I can't change that now because he is gone from me forever. So please don't wait til you can't try to fix sometimes its just the little things.

The only time I feel that you shouldn't go back is when there is any form of physical and some mental abuse. I had mental abuse and sometimes that's worse than the physical. My logic in that is physical abuse the wounds heal but the mental is embedded in your memories and is very hard to get rid of.

I never had any form of physical abuse and I pray for those who have. Please leave because it's not healthy for you or them. And they will never stop.

Once it starts. You are no one's punching bag they sell those in the store. And if you fear being along don't just pray and God will replace what was lost with someone better. And also know it's okay to be alone.

That goes for men as well there are women abusers too. I have seen it myself. I watched a man get hit by his girlfriend socked in front of everyone and he did nothing. Men get away from those kind of women please.

Cause the more you allow her to do that she sees you as week not a leader. She will only get a man that would not allow her to do that and she will show and give him more respect.

That's not okay even if you was told not to hit a women, that doesn't give her the right to hit you. Women these men hurt too so stop it.

WHEN

When will love come for me am I not worthy. I see the mirror image of what I want my life to be. Yet I cry when I see the reflection looking back at me. I close my eyes, opening them up only to this illusion of finding a love that would protect me as his <u>own. One</u> who would guide me and lead me my king. I found him, but when would he find me? When you find the man of your dreams, what do you do? Shall I tell him or keep him as my fantasy? It's something about him when I see him, just a picture. Wow, I am in love with the man in the picture. How could this be. It's silly of me to think that he could even love me. When I see others in love, I am proud to call her his. When will someone be proud to call me theirs? I am cute, in some eyes, fine, smart,witty, loving, and kind, but when you don't have the love from the one you need and want, that when becomes a lifetime. So I sit still and ask God when? The smile that's captivating is attached to a man who stole my heart away all from just one look. Sexy, fine, a leader of many woo, yet I saw the tears in his eyes yearning for a love like mine that only I have to give. A much younger man but a capable man, what would he see in me? It's not what he sees in me, but "WHEN".

INVISIBLE

To be invisible is a lonely place damn, I thought I was seen, but my reality is he never knew I even existed. Looking at you just from a picture, your soul opened wide. Your smile is as beautiful and bright as the sun, the twinkle in your eyes as bright as the Illumination of the brightest star. My protector, my hero, that's what you are to me. When you go and fight battles of war fearless and Wise like the bald eagle. To be invisible is where I don't want to be. Why can't he see me? for although I am broken, but I'm not afraid to keep trying.

Damn how long is it gonna take for you to feel my spirit? when I see you ; you leave me breathless. They say sex is a soul exchange, when the truth is you suck my soul out of me every time I hear you speak. Yet, for now, you still don't see me. I am invisible.

Lavetta Price

CATFISH THE POEM

Alone, lonely, confused, betrayed, misunderstood, hurt pain, decived. Questions unanswered. Why, wondering how did I get here? I am smarter than that, my spirit, Is stronger than that, yet I allowed this fool to catfish me. Damn. Sadly, what I thought was real the real never even had a chance to know me. Fuck wasted time, money. Trust, loyalty all for a fuck boy. Why me? I ASKED MYSELF OVER AND OVER AND OVER AGAIN. Why was I so gullible why I allowed my need and want for love to take me back to where I just came from and never wanted to be. Damaged more so now. God has a way of teaching lessons mine was always continued to listen to my spirit it never failed me his lesson is you never know when God will place someone in your life as a blessing and when you misuse that blessing it has now became your curse. So my deep apologies to the real man and his wife should he have one. I mean no disrespect, but the man in the picture my soul was meant to be, but the man on the phone decieved me. So I came from afar to finally meet the beautiful man I know his soul to be just to see that he is real maybe just a hug to say it's alright not EXPECTING no more then just a simple hello is it me your looking for. One thing for sure, real or fake, neither will you ever forget me, for I am a true gift and a blessing from Jehovah above, and I, too, am safe in God's hands. Amen Thank you.

LaVetta Price

STORY TIME

Sophie had always dreamed of a fairytale wedding - a grand ceremony, a beautiful gown, and a romantic getaway. But as she grew older, she realized that marriage wasn't for her. She loved her independence, her freedom, and her solo adventures. One day, she met Alex, a charming and understanding man who shared her views on marriage.
They fell deeply in love, and Sophie knew she wanted to spend a special day with him - but not a lifetime.
"Let's have a wedding, not a marriage," which goes with the title, so she proposed to Alex.

Alex was taken aback but eventually understood Sophie's perspective. They planned a beautiful wedding, surrounded by friends and family, with all the trimmings - except for the legal binding contract.

On the big day, Sophie wore a stunning gown, and Alex wore a dashing suit. They exchanged vows, rings, and a romantic kiss. They danced, laughed, and celebrated with their loved ones.

After the wedding, they went on a dreamy honeymoon, exploring exotic islands and enjoying each other's company. They returned home, still in love, but without the pressure of marriage.

Sophie and Alex continued to live their lives to the fullest, traveling, pursuing their passions, and enjoying their independence - together, but not tied down. They proved that love doesn't need a legal contract to be real and beautiful.

Years later, when asked about their unconventional choice, Sophie smiled, "We wanted the wedding magic, not the marriage obligations. We chose love on our own terms." And Alex added, "We're living our fairytale, our way."

So as time passed, Sophie and Alex's relationship continued to flourish. They built a life together, but on their own terms. They traveled, explored new hobbies, and supported each other's dreams. Sophie started her own business, a successful event planning company, and Alex became a renowned photographer. They collaborated on projects, and their work took them to exotic locations.

Their love remained strong, and they never felt the need to conform to traditional societal expectations. They were happy, free, and living their best life.

One day, Sophie's mother asked her, "Don't you ever wish you had a traditional marriage, with a husband and kids?"

Sophie smiled, "Mom, I have everything I need. Alex is my partner, my best friend, and my soulmate. We have a beautiful life, and that's all that matters."

Alex overheard the conversation and added, "We're not missing out on anything. We're living our own fairy tale, and it's perfect for us."
Sophie's mother nodded, finally understanding her daughter's unconventional choice. "I just want you to be happy, dear. And you clearly are."
Sophie and Alex's love story became a inspiration to others, proof that true love doesn't need a legal contract to be real and lasting.

They continued to live their life to the fullest, enjoying every moment, and every adventure that came their way.

Written by Best selling Author, a poet that was once told he was not a poet, yet he went on to write a phenomenal book of poetry.

Chinese Proverb

A Chinese Proverb says,
"A man who loves many women, loves none.
But a man who loves one woman loves all."